Cambridge Elements

Elements in Musical Theatre
edited by
William A. Everett
University of Missouri-Kansas City

THE REVUE IN TWENTIETH-CENTURY BUDAPEST

From Cosmopolitan Nightclubs to Stalinist Dogma

Dániel Molnár
Independent Researcher

Shaftesbury Road, Cambridge CB2 8EA, United Kingdom

One Liberty Plaza, 20th Floor, New York, NY 10006, USA

477 Williamstown Road, Port Melbourne, VIC 3207, Australia

314–321, 3rd Floor, Plot 3, Splendor Forum, Jasola District Centre, New Delhi – 110025, India

103 Penang Road, #05–06/07, Visioncrest Commercial, Singapore 238467

Cambridge University Press is part of Cambridge University Press & Assessment, a department of the University of Cambridge.

We share the University's mission to contribute to society through the pursuit of education, learning and research at the highest international levels of excellence.

www.cambridge.org
Information on this title: www.cambridge.org/9781009494458

DOI: 10.1017/9781009298155

© Dániel Molnár 2025

This publication is in copyright. Subject to statutory exception and to the provisions of relevant collective licensing agreements, no reproduction of any part may take place without the written permission of Cambridge University Press & Assessment.

When citing this work, please include a reference to the DOI 10.1017/9781009298155

First published 2025

A catalogue record for this publication is available from the British Library

ISBN 978-1-009-49445-8 Hardback
ISBN 978-1-009-29819-3 Paperback
ISSN 2631-6528 (online)
ISSN 2631-651X (print)

Additional resources for this publication at www.cambridge.org/Molnar

Cambridge University Press & Assessment has no responsibility for the persistence or accuracy of URLs for external or third-party internet websites referred to in this publication and does not guarantee that any content on such websites is, or will remain, accurate or appropriate.

For EU product safety concerns, contact us at Calle de José Abascal, 56, 1°, 28003 Madrid, Spain, or email eugpsr@cambridge.org

The Revue in Twentieth-Century Budapest

From Cosmopolitan Nightclubs to Stalinist Dogma

Elements in Musical Theatre

DOI: 10.1017/9781009298155
First published online: April 2025

Dániel Molnár
Independent Researcher
Author for correspondence: Dániel Molnár, danielmolnarphd@gmail.com

Abstract: Since the introduction of modern revues in 1925, the genre faced near-constant political scrutiny in Budapest. Yet by the 1930s, the city had become the capital of Central European cosmopolitan nightlife. The closure of Hungary's borders after World War II ended any hope of reclaiming this international status. Under communism and the Stalinist totalitarian regime, the revue – despite its popularity – remained politically stigmatised. For the first time, entertainment was treated as a cultural matter rather than merely a law enforcement issue, but it was forced to conform to ideological expectations. Three attempts to legitimise the genre in the 1950s ultimately failed, shaping the trajectory of live entertainment in the era. By the 1960s, revues were officially accepted, yet their cultural significance had faded amid the rise of new entertainment forms.

Keywords: Central European entertainment, popular culture and politics, Cold War cultural history, theatre historiography, entertainment and ideology

© Dániel Molnár 2025

ISBNs: 9781009494458 (HB), 9781009298193 (PB), 9781009298155 (OC)
ISSNs: 2631-6528 (online), 2631-651X (print)

Contents

1	Sources, Methods, Contexts	1
2	From Local Importance to International Fame: 'Budapest Broadway', 1920–1944	5
3	Revues in Crisis	22
4	The Socialist Revue Experiments	37
5	Changes in Set and Costume Design: The Politics of Visual Representation	50
6	The Recuperation and Stabilisation of Revues in Socialist Hungary after 1953	59
7	Epilogue: The Legacy of the Stalinist-Era Revue in Hungary	72
	References	77

1 Sources, Methods, Contexts

While other theatrical genres from Central Europe are receiving increased scholarly attention,[1] revues, spectacles and variety shows seem to have been largely forgotten. These genres, or variants of them, were considered lower art forms, perhaps for being 'merely' entertaining or because they were not primarily narrative based. The lack of scholarly interest in such repertories is perhaps also due to the difficulties of researching their inherent fluidity – they constantly changed from one performance to the next. Furthermore, sources are hard to find. Librettos and scores are almost all lost. Since each production was created for the moment, preserving materials for posterity was not really a consideration. To analyse a performance, each scene would have to be reconstructed from scratch, something that is impossible due to the lack of information about many of the artists involved and their improvised contributions. Moreover, to understand the aesthetics of the revue, one must be aware of the particular dramaturgy and mechanics associated with its constituent acts, keeping in mind that entertainment is first and foremost a commercial enterprise whose goal is to make money. And whose history is this after all? Does it belong to the shows, the venues, the performers, the managers, the politicians or the audience? The answer certainly depends on the availability and types of sources.

I began working in variety shows at age nine, mostly by torturing Sunday audiences at shopping malls with my various acts. More than a decade later, studying simultaneously at the university and the State Circus School, it occurred to me that hardly anyone knew anything specific about the history of show business in Hungary. To this day, many performers argue that 'one cannot write down such things', but I do not share this view. Certainly, there is not one recipe for success when it comes to revues, variety shows and the like, but patterns and strategies of previous eras can be observed, identified and analysed.

My systematic research into this history began by locating and mapping the available sources in public collections. The Hungarian literature on live entertainment falls into two main categories. First are books published by a specific venue, usually written by public relations managers, not historians.[2] Second are those written by the performers themselves, which constitute much of the literature. These also lack analysis or interpretation; often are tinged with nostalgia and are primarily concerned with telling a good story.[3] The anecdotes rarely reflect on the existential and interpersonal conflicts of professional life;

---

[1] Jansen (2020), Bozó (2022).
[2] In case of Fővárosi Nagycirkusz (Municipal Grand Circus), the early vulgar Marxist narratives are still thriving, ignoring the dictatorship and celebrating the 1960s as a 'golden age' for Hungarian performers.
[3] For example, Gál (2005, 2009), Kalmár (2013, 2015) and Rátonyi (1984, 1987).

whatever the authors themselves did not find interesting or did not fit into their public image is conveniently omitted.[4]

Such works are thus tools for nurturing the public image of their authors. Challenging and deconstructing such narratives can be a risky business, to say the least.

Before 1949, entertainment in Hungary consisted of private businesses. Therefore, surviving sources are very limited and include professional and daily press reports, memorabilia and a couple of memoirs. Many press sources are particularly problematic, since most were paid advertisements from the venues. Independent journalists faced numerous challenges, especially when it came to discussing money, since theatres were secretive about their economic situations. In 1919, when Emil Szomory (1872–1944), a journalist and theatre critic, was writing an article about the Budapest theatre business, he confessed, 'I admit that I tried to collect exact data for this article but every manager answered the same way: the budget of the theatre is not the audience's business because they are judging the theatre on its productions and not its ledger'.[5]

After 1949, performance venues became public institutions, which resulted in there being significant amount of documentation, including tax and company reports, deposited in public archives.[6] During the 1980s, the Hungarian Theatre Institute compiled several catalogues for spoken word and operetta theatres, but regarding show venues, this ground work is mostly still missing (see supplementary material www.cambridge.org/Molnár).[7] Nevertheless, entertainment memorabilia collected by enthusiastic individuals and fans as either physical objects or nowadays as Facebook galleries offer tremendous insights into the entertainment industry. (I have amassed my own collection over the years.)

Collections and archives can reveal only part of this story. I conducted oral history interviews with former practitioners who were part of the socialist transformation and who have since passed away. The most important of these was Béla Karády (1922–2016). He was the director and artistic leader of the first municipal entertainment company to create official socialist revues. I first met Karády in 2013 (when he was ninety-one) through one of his former colleagues.

---

[4] In this regard, the memoirs of singer and performer Ilona Nagykovácsi are an exception. She did not try to hide or overlook the hardships of establishing herself in Budapest show business. See Nagykovácsi (1982).

[5] Emil Szomory: Thália birodalma. *Az Ujság naptára* 1919, p. 104.

[6] Unfortunately, this does not mean that everything can be found. Archival materials for Kultúrkapcsolatok Intézete (Institute of Cultural Relations, 1949–1957), the organisation that managed international cultural affairs, are missing, as they are for Pannónia, the state hotel and catering service company.

[7] These catalogues contain information about a specific venue's productions (date, title, creative team, performers, etc.). The closest ones to the present subject concern Budapest cabaret (Alpár, 1978, 1981) and do not include variety or revue.

I knew his name from the archives but did not suspect that he was still alive. After we met for the first time, we agreed to do so again, and we kept meeting every week or so for the next three years, until his death. Our meetings morphed from interviews into conversations between friends about past and contemporary theatre affairs. He trusted me with stories but certainly did not tell me everything. For instance, it later emerged that as a leader of a Hungarian circus company in the 1970s, he had earned a small fortune through corruption. But luckily, we met at the right moment. Karády said that if I had contacted him twenty years earlier, he definitely would not have responded. Just like my other interviewees, he needed distance and had to reach an age where there would not be consequences for talking openly about this informal layer of Hungarian theatre history. The sixty-year age gap between us was a further advantage; I did not pose any professional competition or threat but, since he did not have children, was someone who could carry on his legacy. He kept almost every document from his forty-year theatre career. I would have not known that these documents existed had I not seen them first in his garage. (See Figure 1.) Among them were several unique librettos, but unfortunately not musical scores, which seem to be forever lost.

The goal of the study is to paint a picture of the cultural relevance of musical spectacles in Budapest and their place in different political–historical contexts

Figure 1 Part of Béla Karády's personal archive in his garage in 2014.

from the 1920s through the late 1960s. The 1950s were a turning point in the genre's history in Hungary and since many sources survive from the time, I will present these years in more detail. The underlying question is this: could the Budapest boulevard tradition fit into the cultural dictates of Hungarian Stalinism? The boulevard tradition dates back to the middle of the nineteenth century. The first large-scale metropolitan entertainment venue, the Somossy Orfeum, opened in 1894. Located on Nagymező utca, a cross-street of the famous avenue Andrássy út, not far from the Opera, the location and the building itself exuded class and quality. The area attracted several other entrepreneurs around the turn of the twentieth century, yet by the end of World War I the street had lost most of its glamour and allure.

The term *pesti Broadway* (Budapest Broadway) began to appear in the 1920s, first as a reference to Rákóczi út, which remains one of the main arterial roads in Budapest. In 1926, the first traffic light in the city was installed along it and various entertainment venues, mostly cinemas and nightclubs, opened on the thoroughfare. However, by the second half of the 1930s, Nagymező utca was again the centre for Budapest entertainment around the former Orpheum. A 100-meter segment of the street has been referred to as 'Budapest Broadway' ever since (see Figure 2). These blocks extended their aesthetic reach to the surrounding parts of the VI and VII districts, where other clubs, cabarets and music halls were located.

The word *revü*[8] was borrowed from the French *revue*, meaning 'review'. From about 1930 to 1950, the term was not only used for grand spectacles but also for anything that in English could be described as a show. Two major types of entertainment venues were emerging at the beginning of the twentieth century: orfeum and mulató. Orpheums (the preferred English spelling) were similar to their foreign counterparts: a theatre with either rows of seats or table service that provided variety shows in two parts, each of which consisted of a series of different acts. Mulató was an umbrella term; in colloquial terms, it covered everything from nightclubs to cabarets regardless of size, and structure, whether or not they offered table service or were indoors or outdoors.[9] They were so numerous that in 1938, the Central Statistics Office reported that 'we will not even attempt to list them'.[10]

All translations in this Element are my own unless otherwise noted. Whenever possible, I refer to studies published in non-Hungarian journals and books. In such cases, their original Hungarian editions are generally more detailed than the translations.

---

[8] According to current academic orthography, this is spelled *revü*.
[9] I will use nightclub here.
[10] Elekes (1938: 183).

Figure 2 Montage of the neon lights in Nagymező utca, the 'Budapest Broadway', in 1938. Fortepan / Károly Danassy 210295.

2 From Local Importance to International Fame: 'Budapest Broadway', 1920–1944

2.1 Budapest Nightlife: Dead and Revived

At the turn of the twentieth century, Budapest was becoming known for its vibrant entertainment culture. Its popularity inspired Béla Zerkovitz's 1907 couplet 'Látta-e már Budapestet éjjel?' (Have you ever seen Budapest by night?)[11] and the first act of Imre Kálmán's 1916 hit operetta, *The Csárdás Princess*, set in a Budapest orpheum. In March 1920, however, a writer for the daily newspaper *Világ* published a two-column obituary for Budapest nightlife, claiming that orpheums and clubs had lost three-quarters of their audiences and that in coffee houses, 'three waiters help take off a guest's coat'.[12]

The years between 1918 and 1920 were especially eventful in Hungary. The Kingdom of Hungary had been on the losing side in a world war, the country had gone through a revolution, a Hungarian Soviet Republic had been established and overthrown and a plundering Romanian occupation had transpired. As sa result of the 1920 Treaty of Trianon, Hungary lost two-thirds of its former territory and

---

[11] The song's refrain features the lyrics: 'Have you ever seen Budapest by night? / Come with me and see it with your own eyes! / Don't waste your nights with sleeping in your bed, / That's the way you get to know the real Pest!' *Dezső Gyárfás: Látta-e már Budapestet éjjel?* Dacapo-Record – O-5160, ca. 1908.

[12] N.N.: A pesti éjszaka halála. *Világ*, 21 March 1920, p. 5.

3.3 million Hungarians became minorities in other states. The Kingdom of Hungary was subsequently reinstated, though without a monarch. Miklós Horthy (1868–1957), the last commanding admiral of the Austro-Hungarian navy, served as regent until 15 October 1944. A right-wing authoritarian system was established to curtail the socio-political turbulence of the previous years.[13]

The mood of the 1920s was shaped by the trauma of the treaty. A crisis of cultural identity ensued: what did it mean to be 'Hungarian'? Entertainment, which was viewed as debauchery and part of a frivolous lifestyle, was condemned by politicians on both sides: the left claimed to 'prioritise social welfare' over entertainment, while the right was opposed to the entertainment industry in the name of 'Christian morals'.[14] Entertainment was set against the 'honest, real institutions of culture' (e.g., spoken plays), and the sphere was further demonised after cocaine and morphine began to appear in club culture around 1924.[15] On the other hand, taxes on the entertainment sector generated significant income for the city of Budapest.[16]

Problems with the entertainment industry, however, dominated. The perceived need for 'moral control' of orpheums, cabarets and nightclubs was tied to antisemitic sentiments,[17] and even though show business was not responsible for the coal or apartment shortages, the idea of a wasteful nightlife (and the associated image of those who could afford it) became a perfect scapegoat for social ills. Government-mandated closing hours, higher taxes and another wave of the Spanish flu also negatively affected nightlife. Furthermore, several leading founders – managers of the previous era (e.g., Dezső Gyárfás, Dezső Bálint, Imre Waldmann) died during the decade.

Very few people could afford a night out. In the 1920s, Budapest was a city of refugees and poverty; it did not take much to get beaten or stabbed at night. Due to immigrant and employment crises, many newcomers had to work at night in jobs for which they were often overqualified.[18] The main clientele for nightclubs, the middle class, if they were not working at night, could afford only

---

[13] Gyáni (2004: 492–495).
[14] Miklós Forgács, MP of the Smallholders' Party, demanded: 'Please eliminate this sort of culture, at least for the time being'. 21 July 1922, Nemzetgyűlési Napló 1922/II p. 238.
[15] Budapest éjjeli életébe bevonul a kokain. Pesti Napló, 16 November 1924, p. 7.
[16] In 1921, such taxes generated 50 million Korona. Nándor Bernolák, Minister of Public Welfare, 29 December 1921, Nemzetgyűlési Napló 1920/XIV p. 222. The entertainment tax (*vigalmi adó*) was introduced in 1916 to support social affairs and welfare. Orpheums had one of the highest rates, 25 per cent of the entrance fee (nightclubs were even higher). A similar situation appeared in the 2000s with the rise of ruin pubs.
[17] *Numerus clausus Act,* 1920: XXV. The act formally placed limits on the number of minority students allowed at universities. Although the text did not use the term 'jew', jews were just about the only group overrepresented in terms of higher education. This is often seen as the first antisemitic policy in twentieth-century Europe.
[18] Gyula Lukács: Orvosok mint parkettáncosok ... *Színházi Élet*, 18 April 1920, p. 26.

orpheum entertainment, which, since it was not tied to food and drink, was less expensive. Many journalists at the time saw the middle-class situation as the reason Budapest nights were silent.[19] As Andor Kellér, a well-renowned journalist and writer of the time, put it:

> Abroad, if someone goes out to have fun, they devote a certain sum to having a good night. Money that is not for anything else, that is not supposed to cover the tailor's bill. ... The difference is that the Budapest audience does not spend its spare money at the clubs but instead on the down payment on the fur, the rent, the gas bill and the tuition for a young student. ... Historians of the future will understand Budapest nights ... from this adage: 'Oh my God, if we could live the way we're living.'[20]

Night-time entertainment began to belong to the aristocracy, especially its young people, including teenagers.[21] Clubs became places for the young rich elite to meet, venues where one's behaviour was now less bound by customs and protocol than had previously been the case.[22] This change is likely rooted in the fact that the aristocracy no longer had the political clout to justify its extravagant lifestyle.[23]

Politicians saw many of these cultural challenges as clashes between the 'Hungarian' and the 'foreign' and thought that genres and styles considered 'traditionally Hungarian' must be defended at all costs. This viewpoint was especially evident when it came to the increased popularity of jazz in Hungary, a style that was regarded as the antithesis of traditional 'Hungarian Gypsy music' and a threat to it.[24]

When Imre Magyari and his Gypsy Band were denied permission to perform in London (though they played in Liverpool),[25] the Ministry of Internal Affairs saw an opportunity to influence the Budapest music scene. The Ministry proposed an edict banning foreign musicians from performing in Hungary and expelling the sixteen (Black) jazz musicians then playing in the city. The possible repercussions, namely that Hungarian artists and musicians would likewise be banned abroad, prevented the edict from being as restrictive as originally planned.[26] Another new edict regulating the employment of foreign

---

[19] A pesti éjszaka halála. *Világ*, 14 February 1922, p. 6.
[20] Andor Kellér: Fotográfia a csillogó pesti éjszakáról. *Ujság*, 11 November 1928, p. 10.
[21] Csak szombaton és vasárnap mulat Budapest. *8 Órai Ujság*, 8 December 1925, p. 6. As Count Theodore Zichy remembered, he was only fourteen when he first visited a nightclub – chaperoned by his Jesuit chaplain. See Zichy (1974: 11).
[22] Odeschalchi (1987: 184).   [23] Gyani (2004: 312).
[24] See Zipernovszky (2020). This cultural debate served as a subject for Imre Kálmán's 1928 operetta, *A chicagói hercegnő* (The Duchess of Chicago).
[25] The details of what happened are unclear. Magyar cigányzenészek ... *Az Est*, 1 December 1925, p. 5.
[26] The 281.000/1925 edict about the revision of edicts regarding foreigners. Magyarországi Rendeletek Tára 1925, p. 349

artists introduced an elaborate and off-putting bureaucratic process for both managers and artists 'to defend the workplaces of Hungarian workers'.[27]

Another major cultural challenge related to the Hungarian-foreign question took place in the operetta realm. In 1922, the American theatre entrepreneur Ben Blumenthal acquired the Fővárosi Orfeum (Municipal Orpheum; opened in 1894) and reopened it as Fővárosi Operettszínház (Municipal Operetta Theatre). The change was closely watched. The professional organisation of non-actor performers, Magyarországi Artisták Egyesülete (Association of Artists in Hungary, MAE), mourned the loss of the first music hall in Budapest, since the new profile meant lost work opportunities for its members.[28] Many politicians considered theatre as a tool for creating and nurturing national identity,[29] so it was easy to interpret Blumenthal's actions as a corruption of Hungarian culture.

In 1924, Blumenthal attempted to introduce a business model similar to those of Broadway theatres and Parisian music halls. Instead of having several rotating productions per season, only one production would be staged at a time, a large-scale feast that could hopefully run for years. The first of these was *Halló, Amerika!* (Hullo, America!), which opened on 30 January 1925 and was introduced in the press as representing a new genre: the revue.[30] This production revived the antisemitic sentiments against Blumenthal in the right-wing press and again set up an opposition between 'Hungarian' (operetta) and 'foreign' (revue) genres and cultures. Meanwhile, theatre-sponsored articles and liberal journalists argued that staging a revue was raising Budapest to the level of other European capitals, although they ignored the intercultural conflicts and brutal behaviour of the show's American director. The star performers stood against the revue approach because its real protagonists were the chorus girls and the spectacle – not them.[31] *Halló, Amerika!* was a financial flop. The Budapest audience could not keep the show running for even six months, particularly during this time of hyperinflation. Despite losing money and the political hysteria surrounding it, *Halló, Amerika!* was a spectacle of previously unexperienced size and quality in Hungary and had an enormous cultural

---

[27] 204.000/1925 edict about the regulation and entry of foreign workers. Magyarországi Rendeletek Tára 1925, p. 281.

[28] Róbert Roland: Fővárosi Orfeum. *Artisták Lapja*, 8 September 1921, p. 3.

[29] See Heltai (2022: 167).

[30] The concept was not entirely new in Budapest, though it was rare. The 1906 production of *Madár Matyi* was intended to be such a spectacle. Written by Jenő Heltai and Ferenc Molnár, who later redeveloped the character and story into *Liliom*, it became the eventual basis for *Carousel* (1945) by Richard Rodgers and Oscar Hammerstein II.

[31] Erzsi Péchy, a star of the show, publicly expressed her disapproval: 'The revue? What shall I say? If I said I like it, that wouldn't be true. I was meant to be an operetta actress and I would like to remain one; this new genre … is not for me'. A függöny mögött. *Esti Kurír*, 30 January 1925, p. 9. For an analysis of the production and the debates surrounding it, see Molnár (2021).

impact. In the months that followed, *Halló, Amerika!* was referenced, copied and parodied in Hungarian-language theatres inside and outside Hungary. The show introduced Budapest to the concept of modern revues, added the technical term *görl* (showgirl) to the everyday Hungarian vocabulary and popularised the idea of a show business career for young women.

The question of whether revues could become 'Hungarian' was still being asked at the end of the decade. In 1928, the Operetta Theatre attempted to turn its attention again towards spectacular staging. Mihály Eisemann's *Miss Amerika* featured sixty showgirls, 400 costumes and a camel borrowed from the zoo. The production did not receive any negative reviews; in fact, its run was supported by a press campaign (following the lead of *Halló, Amerika!*), this one celebrating Hungarian invention and fantasy with rumours of a transfer to Vienna or Berlin, though neither happened.[32] An unnamed writer for the *Budapesti Hírlap* (Budapest News) wrote,

> Budapest does not want revues created in the spirit of Western metropolises, but rather Hungarian revues, since Hungarian authors are reformers of the field. Hungarian authors write operetta librettos with a complete story, which they split into scenes and dress in the colourful cloak of the revue.[33]

Although billed as an operetta and having an entirely Hungarian cast and creative team, the key to the show's success was not its narrative elements but rather its staging. Ernő Szabolcs, who directed the production, had worked alongside with Jack Haskell on *Halló, Amerika!* and even inserted a showgirls-on-ladders scene similar to one in the 1925 revue. The production came across as something distinctively 'Hungarian' in a modern, cosmopolitan style. It was the success of the year and established Eisemann as an operetta composer.

Around 1925, things slowly began to change in nightclub culture. It was again safe to be out at night thanks to the bright newly installed neon-lit advertisements. The pre-war *békebeli* (peace time) nightlife had become a subject of nostalgia,[34] and from 1927, the IBUSz (Tourism Office) organised night-time bus tours around the city that included visits to four clubs.[35] The former coffee house in the building of the Operetta Theatre was remade into a luxury nightclub with the name Moulin Rouge. Its parquet floor was covered with crystal glass illuminated from below, providing a unique atmosphere.

---

[32] A Miss Amerika Berlinben. *Esti Kurír*, 5 March 1929, p. 9.
[33] Családfenntartó oroszlán ... *Budapesti Hírlap*, 9 January 1929, p. 11.
[34] For example, Zerkovitz composed another nostalgic song, 'Hol vanrak azok a rég csókos pesti éjszakák?' (Where are those old kissing Budapest nights?) for the January 1928 show at the Royal Orfeum.
[35] Megmutatják az idegeneknek ... *Ujság*, 30 July 1927, p. 6.

With the political consolidation, debates around the legitimacy of entertainment ceased but not ones about its content. In 1927, the Minister of Internal Affairs introduced a moral edict, instructing the police to increase control over all public performances.[36] The edict targeted primarily Budapest. It was daunting and far-reaching and penalised certain individual behaviours. Swearing in public and 'dancing publicly in a way that offends good taste' were prohibited. In the following months, nightclub posters found to be 'indecent' were removed, and a production of *Finom kis lakás* (*Poulet de luxe* by Auguste Achaume) at the Operetta Theatre was even closed. The edict was ridiculed in both the Hungarian and the international press, especially after a bookstore was prosecuted for putting a book in the shop window with Venus de Milo on its cover.[37] The edict was never revoked but the enthusiasm for following it faded into indifference within a couple of years. Among its long-term results, it decreased the respect towards the police (which followed the edict) and the number of syphilis cases rose due to secret prostitution.[38]

The edict's effect came to the fore when the international superstar Josephine Baker (1906–75) included Budapest on her first Central European tour. Her April 1928 performances at the Royal Orfeum and the Moulin Rouge met with loud resistance from conservative politicians on both racial and moral grounds.[39] This was a delicate issue because she had signed a contract with the Royal Orfeum, a private business, with which the government attempted to interfere. She agreed to have a closed 'exam' performance for high-ranking police officers and Ministry officials, who in the end did not chastise her performance. One of them even remarked, 'I've seen several more naked dancers than this!'[40] The political hysteria generated around Baker's visit only enhanced the singer's popularity, which resulted in her shows selling out faster than they would have otherwise. At her fourth public performance, a group of university students threw stench bombs into the audience, but this was the only disturbance during her stay.[41] An added benefit of the hysteria was that Béla Zerkovitz, manager of the Royal Orfeum, composed an advertising foxtrot, 'Gyere, Josephine' (Come Josephine), which became one of the singer's standards when she performed it

---

[36] 151.000/1927. Edict about the protection of public morals. *Magyarországi Rendeletek Tára*, 1927, p. 185.

[37] Suppression of swearing – Humours of a Hungarian crusade. *Observer*, 27 February 1927, p. 12.; Les Hongrois ne badient pas avec l'amour. *Paris-Midi*, 17 March 1927, p. 1. Der Schutz der Moral in Ungarn. *Neues Wiener Tagblatt*, 5 March 1927, p. 8.

[38] Ismét emelkedett Magyarországon ... *Esti Kurír*, 1 January 1931, p. 7.

[39] For Gyula Petrovácz's remarks in the Chamber of Representatives on 25 April 1928, see Képviselőházi Napló, 1927, XI. p. 288.

[40] Josephine Baker 'vizsgaelőadása' a főkapitány előtt. *Pesti Napló*, 1 May 1928, p. 14.

[41] She does not mention any of these events in her memoirs.

in French as 'Dis-moi Joséphine'.[42] Politicians took no notice of her return the next year nor her third visit in 1934.

One of the venues where Baker performed, the Royal Orfeum, dubbed the 'National Theatre of Artists', opened in 1908. It was the largest music hall in Budapest with roughly 1,000 seats, similar in capacity to the Operetta Theatre. Its variety show format did not change significantly over the years: twelve to fourteen acts, split into two parts with an intermission. The programme changed monthly. Since Zerkovitz was keen on engaging the biggest names, all the major continental artists appeared, including the comic acrobats Rivel Brothers, the juggler Rastelli, the clown Grock, the French *vedette* Mistinguett and the magician Okito. In 1929, Zerkovitz attempted to shift from variety shows to revues, but abandoned the idea after just one production, *Start!* The show only ran for a month, and a year later Zerkovitz gave up managing the theatre in order to prevent further losses. This had nothing to do with the aforementioned cultural dispute: the Hungarian quality of his shows was never an issue. It was because he realised that people in Budapest could not afford the high ticket prices that were necessary in order to pay these stars and sustain the theatre long term.[43]

The new manager, Mihály Schmidt, came from the circus industry and implemented a different business model. He aimed for cheap entertainment with two shows a day.[44] But while this was possible for circuses and sideshows in outlying districts, the Royal was a major theatre with significant running costs and a different, multi-layered audience. Within a couple of months, Schmidt decided to also engage music hall stars, including the juggler Sylvester Schäffer Jr, the magician Kassner and the international dancing sensation Marika Rökk. Schmidt shifted his focus in 1932 by booking touring spectacles such as *Doorlay's Non-Stop Revue Tropical Express*[45] and a Viennese hit, *Küsst österreichische Frauen* (Kiss Viennese Women). His biggest success, however, was an original production, *Tessék beszállni!* (All Aboard!), in 1933 (see Figure 3.).[46] Schmidt's major source of revenue was renting out the theatre for boxing and wrestling matches, since Budapest did not have a dedicated, suitable venue for such events. The Royal Orfeum was still far from profitable, and Schmidt went bankrupt. He gave up the house in 1934 to pay off his debts and for treatment for the health issues he developed during his managerial years. Although he, like Zerkovitz, tried several

---

[42] Baker performed the song in the 1930 revue of Casino de Paris, *Paris qui remue* (Paris in motion) and used it for the title of her 1955 album.
[43] A Royal Orfeumot a jelenlegi... *Pesti Napló*, 11 March 1930, p. 15.
[44] Schmidt Mihály 'kilovagolt' a Royal Orfeumból. *Magyarország*, 5 May 1934, p. 15.
[45] On the Berlin performance, see Lewerenz (2014).
[46] The show was set on an ocean liner – a year before Cole Porter's *Anything Goes* premiered on Broadway. It ran for 133 evenings and inspired a way less successful sequel the same year: Tessék kiszállni! [Everyone off!].

Figure 3 Playbill cover for *Tessék beszállni!* (All aboard!) by Alfréd Márkus, starring Lici Balla.

different artistic-business strategies, none of them worked. The problem was the financially strapped Budapest population, an insolvable dilemma.

The 1930s were a critical period not only for variety shows and revues but also for the so-called national genre, the 'Hungarian' operetta, which was almost fetishised a few years earlier. The Operetta Theatre went bankrupt in 1935. *Én és a kisöcsém* (Me and My Little Brother) by Mihály Eisemann had been a success the previous year,[47] but due to the management's overall

---

[47] The production opened on 21 December 1934.

financial instability, the flop of the next production, *Grand Café*, was enough to put the theatre out of business. The same thing happened to the other major operetta theatre in town, the Király Színház (Király Theatre). Its final decade existed in complete agony, with six different managements in eleven years. After it closed in 1936, several luminaries reflected on the operetta crisis, looking beyond the lack of capital. The playwright and humourist István Békeffi claimed that the spread of movies with synchronised sound (talkies) had resulted in a loss of audiences for operettas.[48] Sándor Incze, the editor-in-chief of the most influential theatre magazine, *Színházi Élet* (Theatre Life), blamed the decline on a lack of stars, who either chose better-paying foreign engagements or emigrated.[49] The operetta historian Gyöngyi Heltai asserts that social attitudes also played a major role. The political elite did not separate operetta from national culture but neither did they make any efforts to sustain the genre. Neither audiences and critics nor performers supported the attempted changes in style. Budapest audiences demonstratively rejected the modern stagings that alluded to contemporary domestic and foreign affairs. These were not what audiences expended. They clearly preferred nostalgia-tinged productions and disliked any attempts to modernise either the content or the form of the genre.[50]

Despite financial losses and critical failures, entrepreneurial enthusiasm remained high. After every bankruptcy there were potential leaseholders for empty theatres, Hungarians and foreigners alike. Bernardo Labriola, the manager of the Ronacher Theater in Vienna, attempted to expand his business in Budapest by opening a music hall. Likely inspired by the German concept of *Großvarieté* (producing variety-style shows for audiences of 3,000), in 1932 he took over the largest theatre in the city, the Városi Színház (City Theatre), which had about 2,000 seats. The plan did not work; his venture folded the next year. In July 1935, Teddy (István) Ehrenthal, a Hungarian agent with theatrical interests in Paris, announced that he would rent the Operetta Theatre building for six years and run it as a music hall. He renamed it the Fővárosi Orfeum and even managed to engage the Hollywood film star Ramón Novarro to perform there. Ehrenthal, however, became embroiled in a scandal: he did not have the money to pay the contracted artists, fled the country, was arrested in Vienna and extradited to the custody of the Hungarian police.[51] In 1936, Philipp Lesing,

---

[48] István Békeffy: Noé bárkája a színházban. *Színházi Élet*, 19 April 1936, pp. 13–16.
[49] 'Operetta theatres are closed because Gitta Alpár, Irén Zilahy, Rózsi Bársony, Irén Biller, Marika Rökk, Magda Kun, Erzsi Paál, Oszkár Dénes, (István) Gyergyai were taken abroad'. Ne csak látogatóba jöjjenek haza. *Színházi Élet*, 5 April 1936, p. 12.
[50] Heltai (2011b: 62–64).
[51] Kiadatási eljárás Ehrenthal Teddy ellen. *Magyarország*, 8 September 1937, p. 8.

manager of the Liebig Theater in Breslau (today Wrocław, Poland), reopened the Király Színház as Fővárosi Orfeum. The enterprise lasted two days.

Since theatre entrepreneurs lacked capital, it was impossible for them to run a stable business.[52] Theatre journalist Sándor Incze noted that entrepreneur-managers were not the only ones to blame. One also had to consider the theatre owners: in America, the theatre owner even helps out certain talented producers financially. In our midst, they find it natural that a leaseholder candidate sits down to negotiate with only the advance payment of the ticket office, the cloakroom and the buffet in his pocket.[53]

Building owners were more focused on short-term income than on long-term artistic and business goals. By the middle of the 1930s, only occasional summer open-air venues mounted large-scale productions. As *Variety* put it:

> Not one big vaudeville or variety theatre has been playing in Budapest for years. Instead, night club (sic) floor shows have attained a very high standard and unequalled popularity.[54]

It is to these nightclubs we now turn our attention.

2.2 World-Famous Wonder Bars

During the 1930s, Budapest's show business reached international fame in the Western world through its luxurious nightclubs. Apart from the experience and business acumen of a new generation of managers, international circumstances were in its favour. After Hitler rose to power in 1933, the liberal and (in-)famous Berlin club culture of the 'goldene Zwanziger' (the golden twenties) was over. Budapest, traditionally considered to be on the edge of Western Christian culture, provided an exotic setting where a night out was significantly cheaper than elsewhere in Europe. By 1935, it offered a wide selection of high-quality spectacles. Nightclub shows were not new, but their scale and quality reached new levels. Shows were reviewed in *Variety* and *Billboard* and by the continental press. Foreign papers highlighted their cosmopolitan nature, while Hungarian ones emphasised their local value. Smaller clubs billed themselves as *világvárosi szórakozóhely/műsor* (global city venue/show), implying nostalgically that Budapest was still a centre of cultural-political influence.[55] The

---

[52] 'Every day for a long while now such theatre enterprises were created which did not have any other capital except leasing the cloakroom and the buffet. They took loans, employed actors, craftsmen and tradesmen who lost their offset ... due to the fact that these ventures did not have proper coverage'. Sajtópör a Fővárosi Operettszínház összeomlása miatt. *Az Est*, 12 December 1935, p. 4.

[53] Hiányzik a varieté. *Színházi Élet*, 9 February 1936, p. 18.

[54] No Budapest Vaude. *Variety*, 22 May 1934, p. 49.

[55] The population of Budapest in 1935 was around one million, nowhere near that of metropolises like Berlin, Paris or London. Even Vienna had twice as many inhabitants as Budapest.

interior design of clubs was a cardinal question. Aside from being functional, the decor had to create a distinctive atmosphere, one which also served as a permanent set for the stage shows[56] (see Figures 4 and 5). For example, the

Figure 4 Postcard showing the interior of the Aranypók (Golden Spider) Dancing, 1942. Message: 'To Miss Márti Benedek / I'm writing to you from this dark place where we entered in a sudden confusion. I'm thinking a lot about you. (Bandi and the others did not dare to enter.) Kisses, Ernő Dénes Asztalos'.

---

[56] Only major clubs, like the Moulin Rouge, had a dedicated stage. The priority was to maximise the number of guests.

Figure 5 Postcard showing the interior of the Jardin d'Atelier, 1936.

Jardin d'Atelier was inspired by a French village, while the Sanghay was richly decorated with chinoiserie and the Capri evoked a dripstone cave. Major clubs also ran summer venues either on Margaret Island (e.g., the Parisien Grill from 1931) or in the Városliget (City Park). Open-air clubs like the Plantage Bar or the Jardin de Paris were only open during the summer months.

Although the Minister of Commerce expressed that Budapest, besides its spas, should be known as 'the city of entertainment',[57] this did not mean that nightlife would be supported by the state or the municipality in any way. Nonetheless, 'Budapest Broadway' and its clubs appeared in official tourist pamphlets and guidebooks.

In 1931, after the suicide of the previous manager, Ernő Flaschner took over the Moulin Rouge. Like him, many of the new entrepreneurs had worked as waiters in the 1920s before they opened their own clubs.[58] Flaschner assembled a more or less permanent production team to provide interactive spectacles for his guests. He considered his venue a theatre; at its peak, a cast and crew of 120 were involved with the shows, which he called *lokálrevű* (nightclub revue).[59]

Another manager, Sándor Rozsnyai, began his career as a musical parodist and conductor. He had a double act with his wife, who was known by her stage name, 'Miss Arizona'. After touring for about fifteen years, in 1932, they bought the

---

[57] Tihamér Fabinyi: A Turista Szövetség teremtse meg az idegenforgalom parlamentjét. *Turistaság és Alpinizmus*, March 1934, p. 59.
[58] Orlay (1943: 42–43). The spread of ruin pubs happened in a similar way in the early 2000s.
[59] Ernő Flaschner: A Moulin Rouge revüinek története. *Artisták Lapja*, December 1939, p. 4.

house opposite the Moulin Rouge, in which they opened the Arizona Revue Dancing.[60] Miss Arizona was the star of productions, although her artistry was not the main draw. Their shows relied primarily on the acts featuring the showgirls – who at one point were hanging upside down from a chandelier – and the theatre's technology. The main attraction was the revolving parquet dance floor, which could also be lowered and raised. Furthermore, the side boxes could be hidden with the push of a button. In 1935, the couple launched a marketing campaign using the word *csodabár* (wonder bar), an *epitheton ornans* which they used, and others copied until the end of World War II.[61]

By 1935, the Arizona Revue Dancing and the Moulin Rouge could each accommodate about 200 guests, which in the case of the Moulin Rouge doubled by 1943.[62] Their business models were similar: entrance was free, though purchasing food and drink was expected and encouraged.[63] Both clubs relied heavily on the objectification and extreme exploitation of young women. Several similar venues tolerated prostitution, both male and female.[64] A double standard regarding public morals existed: while nudity and sexualisation were explicit on stage and in the playbills, the first Hungarian 'men's lifestyle magazine', the Playboy-like *Új Magazin* (New Magazine) was banned from publishing such pictures taken by the same photographer. Both clubs produced a new show every month, unless the previous one was so popular that it was extended. At the Moulin Rouge, shows began around 10 p.m. and the second part started after midnight; the Arizona Revue Dancing advertised itself with 'a new attraction every 15 minutes'. In 1937, a Moulin Rouge playbill was 64 (!) pages long. While the Arizona's was shorter, it was covered in photos. They also served as a souvenir and advertised the venues in four languages (Hungarian, French, English and German; See Figure 6).[65]

The usual closing time for both clubs was 5 a.m. From 1934, on Sundays and holidays, five o'clock teas with a full show – practically matinees – were also offered for those who preferred not to stay out all night. *Mondain* dance novelties – like the beguine, the rumba and several others developed in-house – were introduced in club productions. Between acts, customers danced to the

---

[60] See Molnár (2017).
[61] The expression was not new. It likely came from the eponymous 1930 play by Herczeg-Farkas-Kätscher. A Hollywood film version appeared in 1934, and a year later the play was revived in Budapest.
[62] Floorplan, 12 November 1943, BFL IV. 1420. c. 56. d.
[63] The profit margin on a bottle of *barack* (apricot brandy) in the Arizona was about 93 per cent; however, champagne was the most stable source of income. Sándor Lestyán: A pesti éjszaka és vendégei. *Ujság*, 27 June 1937.
[64] Szántó (1933: 9).
[65] Az éjszaka – La Nuit – The night – Die Nacht; between cca. 1937 and 1939. OSZK SzT Playbill Collection: Moulin Rouge.

Figure 6 Page from the four-language playbill of Arizona Revue Dancing, 1935.

music of Hungarian jazz bands. These bands achieved international fame and were frequently heard on the Budapest Radio and the BBC.[66]

---

[66] *The Duke of Windsor likes this band. Melody Maker*, 23 October 1937, p. 3.

To satisfy demands from both locals and the international clientele, 'Gypsy' bands were also featured. The Moulin Rouge produced the first ethnic-inspired showgirl act in April 1937. It included traditional steps and visual designs and claimed to represent authentic Hungarian folk culture. The concept was copied by every major venue in town, except – significantly – the Arizona.

Originally both the Moulin Rouge and the Arizona targeted the local upper middle class, but by 1935, both became known as regular informal meeting places of the elite, not only the monied but also the politicians.[67] István Bethlen Jr, son of the Prime Minister, fondly remembered his visits to the clubs:

> I think I was the first playboy in Hungary. ... My father was the omnipotent Hungarian Prime Minister and I, his omnipotent son. My father was the friend of (Regent) Miklós Horthy, and I was the best friend of Pista Horthy (his son). So while the old men did the politics, we spent our time in a much smarter way. Oh, pal, those were good times! When Pista Bethlen and Pista Horthy went to a nightclub, every night fairy who was worth something clattered and even the gypsy carrying the double bass stuffed himself with *foie gras* and drank champagne. On my right knee, a blonde was sitting; on the left a brunette, while I was hugging a raven-haired with my left arm and a redhead with my right.[68]

The British fascination with Hungary grew in the late 1920s, thanks largely to Lord Rothermere, who was a loud supporter of Hungarian revisionism.[69] The visit(s) of the Prince of Wales, the future Edward VIII,[70] gave it a further boost. Budapest nightlife became the subject of English-language reports, travelogues and novels.[71] Numerous Hungarian novels were set partially or entirely in nightlife by Erzsébet Barra, Andor Kellér and Tivadar Zichy to name a few. Stage plays and films also capitalised on the subject starting with the second Hungarian talkie, *Hyppolit, a lakáj* (Hyppolit, the Butler, 1931), *Havi 200 fix* (Salary, 200 a Month, 1936) or *Egy nap a világ* (There's Only Today, 1944).[72] A French (*Retour à l'aube*, 1938) and as well as an American film (*As You Desire Me* with Greta Garbo, 1932) were set in Budapest nightclubs. An article in the American fashion magazine, *Vogue* also praised the city's nightlife in March 1939.[73]

---

[67] A state secretary's wild night out was the subject of an article in 1929. Hogy mulat az igazságügyi államtitkár ... *Esti Kurír*, 5 March 1929, p. 3.
[68] Dunai (1984: 132). [69] Cartledge (2011: 343).
[70] Edward (1951: 423). He did not go into detail regarding his four Budapest journeys. He was not the first Prince of Wales to visit the city: in 1888, the future Edward VII also experienced the local entertainment.
[71] For example, Brophy (1936) and Gyn (1932).
[72] The only known documentary about Budapest nightlife is a 1940 short film by János Dáloky, *Látta-e már Budapestet télen?* (Have you ever seen Budapest in Winter?) Two of its sixteen minutes are dedicated to the show at the Arizona Revue Dancing. In the 1951 Fellini-Lattuada film, *Luci del varietà*, the showgirls' trainer was Hungarian.
[73] Bettina Wilson: Budapest. *Vogue*, 1 March 1939, p. 135.

2.3 The Restrained and 'Adjusted' Show Business

The 1938/XV. Act, established to 'secure the balance of social and economic life', became Hungary's first (explicit) anti-Jewish law. It set a maximum percentage of Jews who could participate in public life. A year later, a second anti-Jewish law banned Jews from every position 'which influences the employment of artists or the artistic direction of a theatre'.[74] The 1938 act established various profession-based bodies (called chambers) whose purpose was to exclude Jewish artists and intellectuals. The Színház- és Filmművészeti Kamara (Chamber of Theatre and Film Arts) was charged to 'ensure the demands of national spirit and Christian morals'.[75] The process was referred to as *átállítás* ('adjustment'), but it was clear that the complete and immediate implementation of these laws would have paralysed the theatre and film industries. Far-right and antisemitic papers complained that nightclubs, either through straw men or directly, were still being managed by Jews. Indeed, managers found legal loopholes to keep their businesses. For example, Sándor Rozsnyai registered the Arizona under his wife's name. Shortly afterwards, he was drafted for labour service alongside his son, who died of suicide rather than having to serve.[76]

Ernő Flaschner could have remained in charge of the Moulin Rouge until 1942 and still have employed several Jewish artists. A management change, details of which are unclear, took place. In the end, the far-right sympathising headwaiter-turned-entrepreneur János Nedeczvári replaced Flaschner. The house was renamed its Hungarian equivalent, Vörös Malom, and nationalist overtones were added to the show. Claiming national pride, artists with foreign names were pressured to adopt Hungarian ones.[77] Showgirls had to appear by their given names, for example, Márta Mázik instead of 'La Bella Marta'. This looked particularly grotesque in the case of married women who used their husbands' names; for example, one showgirl was credited as 'Mrs Wiesner'.

Music halls and clubs did not fall under the jurisdiction of the Chamber, which had a hostile attitude towards them. In 1941, the jazz musician Sándor Heinemann managed to successfully reopen the Royal as Revüszínház (Revue Theatre) and produce shows there each month; however, the Chamber protested against the use of the term 'theatre'. In March 1943, its name became Revüpalota (Revue Palace), even though the venue was not a nightclub but a 1,000-seat theatre.[78]

---

[74] 1939, IV. 11. §
[75] For more on the relationship between the Chamber and professional associations, see Heltai (2017).
[76] Szíven lőtte magát ... *Pesti Hírlap*, 17 June 1942, p. 7.
[77] A magyar név fénye. *Artisták Lapja*, 15 October 1942, p. 3.
[78] Letter from Szöllősy, ministerial advisor, to the Mayor, 29 March 1943, BFL IV. 1420. c. 44. d.

The Chamber also influenced the venue's employment policy. The management had to submit a report to the Chamber listing their contracted performers. For the opening production in September 1941, the Chamber only objected to one artist, Ernő Szabó, whose appearance was 'not recommended'.[79] The reason is unknown; Szabó was an established actor from a theatrical dynasty, and his engagement at the Royal had been announced in July.[80] Furthermore, he was a member of the Chamber and had even worked at the Royal the previous season. In 1941, Szabó was a member of the theatre company in Nagyvárad, a Transylvanian town which had been returned to Hungary the previous August. Perhaps the Chamber thought that promoting Hungarian culture in Nagyvárad was more important than an occasional performance in a Budapest music hall. The Chamber's rejection of Szabó's employment arrived only three days before opening night, a verdict that likely caused a severe headache for the management.

The Chamber lobbied each year to take over entertainment venues for their own purposes, but the MAE managed to defend the interests of the artists. (Music hall licences were granted formally by the police on the recommendation of the Chamber.) Many banned Jewish artists, including the operetta star Rózsi Bársony and the comedian István Békeffi, became members of the MAE, which out of solidarity allowed them to keep performing. According to the 1944 report, 150 Jews were among the 2,000 members of MAE.[81] As a result, the association was heavily attacked by the far-right press. The Chamber also lobbied against the MAE, which resulted in the Minister of Internal Affairs ordering that monologues, couplets and solo acts 'belonging to theatre arts' could only be performed by members of the Chamber.[82] The MAE protested against this unreasonable restriction, especially because employment for artists had become very difficult after Hungary entered World War II in the summer of 1941.

On 19 March 1944, the German Reich invaded and occupied the Hungarian Kingdom. The Minister of Internal Affairs immediately closed all theatres and performance venues for a week, during which it reviewed employment records and deposed all Jews from music halls. As a result, several venues closed[83] and remaining ones had significantly fewer customers.[84]

The Hungarian National Socialist force, the Nyilaskeresztes Párt – Hungarista Mozgalom (Arrow Cross Party – Hungarist Movement) had a particular vision for

---

[79] Letter from Károly Vargha to the Presidency of the Chamber of Theatre and Film Arts. 28 August 1941, BFL IV. 1420. c. 44. d.
[80] Egy új színigazgató nyilatkozik. *Ujság*, 18 July 1941, p. 10.
[81] 150 tagot töröl az Artista Egyesület. *Függetlenség*, 6 April 1944, p. 5.
[82] Rendelet az artista előadó számokról. *Magyar Artisták Lapja*, 15 August 1942, p. 3.
[83] Az artista munkahelyek védelmében. *Magyar Artisták Lapja*, 15 May 1944, p 1. See also Átszervezték a varieté-színházakat. *Esti Ujság*, 28 March 1944, p. 6.
[84] Zoltán Nyisztor: Szórakozás a mai időknek. *Nemzeti Ujság*, 16 April 1944, p. 6.

the future of Budapest entertainment. The party's paper, *Magyarság* (Hungarians), proposed transforming music halls into 'literature cabarets with an articulated spirit' led by 'pure Aryan and nationally committed professionals'.[85] Furthermore, the new mayor of did not see the city's nightlife as a defining part of its future:

> This city is in the state of being reborn. Likely, this capital, whose beauty lies in its natural treasures and human creations, will not be famous for having lots of silver-mirrored coffee houses. ... People might say that there are few theatres and few nightclubs. They might. That's all right. The Budapest of the future, the capital of Hungary, should be famous for her other virtues.[86]

Heinemann closed the Royal in April to avoid being accused of employing Jews. The Nazi leisure organisation Kraft durch Freude (Strength through Joy) took over the theatre in June and under the name Magyar-Német Katonaszínház (Hungarian-German Military Theatre) produced opera and variety shows until mid-December 1944, except in September, when the Minister ordered every club and bar closed.[87] This decree of 2 September 1944 came one week after Goebbels announced the closure of German and Czech theatres. Budapest theatres reopened in October, but not the clubs.

On 15 October 1944, Regent Miklós Horthy announced that Hungary had signed a cease-fire with the Soviet Union. Blackmailed by the Nazis along with his son, he renounced the armistice on the same day and abdicated in favour of the Arrow Cross Party leader, Ferenc Szálasi, who became prime minister. The Hungarist Government's authority was limited to the territory around Budapest, and its rule was brutal. Deportations and death squads were commonplace, and the Danube became filled with corpses, including that of the prima donna–entrepreneur Miss Arizona. Her husband was likely killed in a concentration camp. On Christmas Eve, the Soviet siege of Budapest began. When it ended on 13 February 1945, Budapest lay in ruins. Roughly 80 per cent of its buildings were destroyed or damaged, as well as all seven bridges across the Danube.

3 Revues in Crisis

As a result of the war, 40 per cent of Hungary's national wealth was depleted and 6.2 per cent of the population perished. Soviet troops were looting and raping on the streets of Budapest, and plans were being made in Moscow to make the country a Soviet satellite state. Still, the transitional phase that lasted

---

[85] Irodalmi kabarét a varieték és orfeumok helyére! *Magyarság*, 29 March 1944, p. 9.
[86] Emergency meeting of the municipal committee on 14 June 1944. Minute book published in *Fővárosi Közlöny* (Municipal Bulletin), 7 July 1944.
[87] Operaelőadások a 'Kraft durch Freude' színházában. *Esti Ujság*, 17 August 1944, p. 6. cf. Letter of Ferenc Görgey (Ministry of Homeland Defense) to the legal representative of Sándor Heinemann, 11 October 1944, BFL XIV. 265. 3. d.

until 1948–49 was characterised by an economy that still avowed market mechanisms and political–cultural pluralism.[88] In 1946, the Republic of Hungary was declared. The Paris Peace Settlement cemented the borders of the country to their pre-1938 state, repeating the trauma of 1920. The communist takeover accelerated after 1948, and a year later the new constitution established a Soviet-type totalitarian dictatorship under the Magyar Dolgozók Pártja (Hungarian Workers' Party), led by Mátyás Rákosi (1892–1971), known as 'the best pupil of Stalin'. Hungarian society was restructured to destroy 'the bourgeoisie' and marginalise the traditional elite.[89] Heavy industries were prioritised, making Hungary 'the country of iron and steel', and the minimal production of consumer goods resulted in frequent shortages.

3.1 A Dubious Legacy

After the Soviet occupation of Budapest, the Mayor ordered a *tabula rasa* for theatres. Entertainment and its cultural place and role were again being debated at local (municipal) and national (ministerial) levels.[90] The political attitude toward the legacy of club culture and nightlife was hostile, for clubs were still associated with the privileged, so much so, that even representatives of the liberal party were supporting and demanding the investigation of their clientele.[91] The only counter-argument was the financial interest of the city: entertainment and luxury taxes still brought in significant income. After a communist mayor came to power in 1947, the party made a U-turn. They began campaigning for lowering and ultimately abolishing the entertainment tax, but the idea of 'educational productions' was behind this egalitarian approach.[92] Police oversight was normal, although closing times were not always respected by the policemen themselves.[93]

Several clubs reopened after the war, mostly under new managers who were willing to continue the established brands. In such an environment, no new clubs opened. When clubs reopened, they were on a significantly smaller scale than before. The floor shows reflected the changing political-social system, which would not allow any sort of Arizona Revue Dancing- or Moulin Rouge-style enterprise. This went along with the fact that the opulent lifestyle

---

[88] Romsics (1999: 219).   [89] Valuch (2004: 578).   [90] See the details in Molnár (2014).
[91] József Kabakovits, representative of the Civic Democratic Party (*PDP*), at the session of the Public Administration Committee *Fővárosi Közlöny*, 31 December 1946, p. 1463.
[92] Comment of Endre Frey at the regular session of the Municipal Assembly, 24 November 1948. 2nd Appendix to *Fővárosi Közlöny*, 11 December 1948, p. 6.
[93] 'I ordered that every entertainment venue should close at 23:00. My controlling officers on 5 October 1945 found the Casino Café open at 23:30. The manager claimed that there were fifteen detectives from the political department there, hence he could not close. The detectives informed my officers that they were on stakeout and it was their hiding place'. The Ministry of Interior's letter to the political department of the Budapest police, 12 October 1945, MNL OL XIX-B-1-r 20. d.

of their audiences had also disappeared. Furthermore, the new managers lacked the capital and imagination of their predecessors.

Under the new regime, Sándor Heinemann was not allowed to continue managing the Royal because he exposed himself propagating the war.[94] Instead, the licence was given to László Gonda, who was supported by the newly organised trade union of artists. However, even this decision was overturned a couple of months later, and the theatre landed in the hands of Teddy Ehrenthal in acknowledgement of his services translating for the leaders of the Soviet army.[95] His networks and back-room deals turned out to be so much stronger than the lobby of the party-supported trade union that the union had to ignore his criminal past. He held the Royal's licence for the next four years, and in August 1946, acquired a licence to reopen the Moulin Rouge. Its former manager, Ernő Flaschner, survived the war and – perhaps unwillingly – relinquished his contract[96] to the Bureau of Soviet Assets in Hungary.[97]

Singers, comedians, dancers and jazz musicians dominated the nightclub offerings. Sketches ridiculed fascist leaders and politicians, something that had not been allowed publicly for years. Dancers learned new steps seen in Hollywood films, which were being screened until the Stalinist turn. Jazz historian Géza Gábor Simon describes the period between 1945 and 1950 as the 'golden era' of Hungarian jazz: György Cziffra, Jenő (Bubi) Beamter, Lajos Martiny, Mihály Tabányi, Jenő Orlay (Chappy) and several others resumed playing American-style jazz and jazz-influenced dance music in bars and nightclubs.[98]

While clubs were watched closely, music halls were not, and thus they provided spaces for both politically and sexually explicit humour. The productions were targeted primarily at a Hungarian audience – there was hardly any chance to develop international tourism in Budapest at the time due to limited

---

[94] Heinemann composed a military march, *Tiértetek* (For you), for the February 1942 show, which quickly became very popular. However, its staging did not please everyone. A reviewer wrote: 'The military scene of *Tiértetek* is not suited for a revue stage because it is utterly strange when after cannons, soldiers and a big snowy flatland, suddenly a group of . . . girls appear on stage'. Based on this description, its style might have been similar to that of 'Springtime for Hitler' in Mel Brooks's *The Producers*. Bemutató a Royal Revűszínházban. *Népszava*, 5 February 1942, p. 7.
[95] Molnár Gál (2001: 247).
[96] Letter from Ernő Flaschner to the Folyószámla Leszámítolóbank Rt., 6 August 1946, BFL XIV. 265. 3. d.
[97] To prepare for the Sovietisation of the country, several Soviet–Hungarian companies were established by taking over 'German assets'. Their primary focus was to cover strategically important sectors like the navy and air transportation; but due to the takeover, several other companies also became Soviet property, for example, the theme park in the City Park. Letter from János Erőss, president of the War Relief Office, to Marshal Voroshilov, 10 March 1946, BFL VII. 2. e. Angol Park Rt. Cg. 12959. See also Szívós-Uzoni (1992).
[98] Simon (1999: 123–134). See also Simon (1992: 61–63).

transportation options and government bureaucracy,[99] not to mention that the city was in ruins.

Aside from the many theatre artists who were killed, the profession lost others who either did not return to Hungary at the end of the war or left the country before 1949. These included composer Alfréd Márkus, comedian László Békeffi, acrobatic dance groups Trio Mexicanos and Trio Rudas and operetta stars Oszkár Dénes and Rózsi Bársony. The circle of employable artists was narrowed even further to only those approved by the regulatory committees (*igazolóbizottság*), which scrutinised the political past and attitudes of anyone who was publicly or privately employed.[100]

MAE tried to re-establish itself as a trade union in 1945, but the Council of Trade Unions rejected its application.[101] Newly established trade unions functioned as tools of the communist takeover in every sector, and their creation made them easy to fill with the politically trusted as well as to discredit and replace older organisations.[102] MAE members were forced to join the new trade union by making membership a condition of performing in public from May 1947. Nevertheless, the fact that warnings to this effect were printed again and again and even appeared a year later in the professional journal *Artisták Lapja* suggests that in practice the requirement was frequently ignored. Eliminating the networks of theatre and music hall agents also took some time after agencies were taken over by trade unions. Professional artists formed a narrow strand of society that existed through interpersonal networks, which were difficult to control from the outside. Economic interests became stronger than professional solidarity: artists began informing on each other to lessen the competition.[103] MAE was disbanded in 1948, and the transition to Stalinism accelerated.

A press campaign against music halls began that harshly criticised the shows as being harmful and pornographic. Music halls were targeted because they were still privately managed and carried low cultural prestige. The threatening tone of journalists and the clear political messages toward music halls were new items in theatre magazines. For example, István Fejér wrote in the theatre magazine *Színház és Mozi* (Theatre and Cinema):

---

[99] On the necessary bureaucratic steps for entering the country, see Hevesi (1948). The Tourism Office produced pamphlets as early as 1945. The centennial celebrations of the 1848 Revolution and the 1949 World Festival of Youth and Students were the last major tourist events in the country before its isolation.

[100] *Artisták Lapja*, May 1946, p. 2.

[101] Letter of the MAE to the Minister of Internal Affairs, 14 August 1945, OSZK SzT Irattár 3–20.

[102] Magyar Hivatásos Zenészek és Artisták Szabad Szakszervezete (Free Trade Union of Hungarian Professional Musicians and Artists), 1945–1950.

[103] For the reports, see OSZK SzT Irattár 3–20.

Theatre managers, music halls, provincial companies, nightclubs and even provincial and Budapest amateurs produce operettas, comedies and farces from the storage closet of the past, counting on the working masses' desire for pleasantry. ... Lies, intended reactionism, smokescreen, dulling people and destroying their taste. Mental fascism. This characterises that dangerous toxin which poisoned our people for decades and which we still wrongfully overlook and tolerate on the stages of the people's democracy both in Budapest and in the countryside.[104]

He thus removed all forms of boulevard theatre from the future of Hungarian theatre. The Kamara Varieté (Chamber Music Hall) was even accused of being a brothel where shows were only a side hustle. This was despite the fact that it was a theatre with a stage and about 150 seats arranged in rows. Aside from the critical crossfire targeting the shows, managers were often personally attacked in the press, including the formerly politically favoured Teddy Ehrenthal.[105]

3.2 A Close Circle of Friends

The private sector had not completely disappeared by 1949. After the last wave of theatre nationalisation in July, the Municipal Grand Circus, the Royal, the Kamara Varieté and side shows still remained under private management. These venues were so far away from the political spotlight that the official Party proposal for a new theatre structure did not even mention them.[106]

That situation, however, would soon change. The Municipal Council proposed the creation of a new municipal company, Fővárosi Népszórakoztató Intézmények (Municipal Institutions of People's Entertainment, FŐNI). The goal of the new initiative was 'to raise standards regarding cultural policy'.[107] The cadre of ambitious young people responsible for the proposal sought to take over the remaining parts of the entertainment sector.

One of the leading forces behind FŐNI was Béla Karády (1922–2016), the only child of a Jewish middle-class family. Bitten by the theatre bug as a child, from an early age he was writing reviews and playing 'filmmaking' with his friends. Karády had been a *bocher*[108] but gave up his rabbinical studies to study mathematics and art history at university. He began his theatre career as a prompter for the Jewish cultural association's (OMIKE) theatre performances around 1939–40. In 1944, he was deported to the Mauthausen concentration

---

[104] A népellenes könnyű műfaj. *Színház és Mozi*, 6 April 1949, p. 12.
[105] '(Since) Teddy Ehrenthal is the omnipotent master of Royal Revü Varieté, the spirit of fascist detention camps, social exploitation and the harshest tone is ruling the theatre'. Ehrenthal Teddy rémuralma ... *Színház és Mozi*, 4 May 1949, p. 8.
[106] Proposal to nationalise Budapest theatres. n. d. (1949), MNL OL M-KS 276. f. 109. cs.
[107] Proposal to municipalise entertainment venues. n. d. (1949), MNL OL M-KS 276. f. 109. cs.
[108] Borrowed from the Yiddish בחור, a rabbinical student.

camp. After his return to Budapest in 1946, he secured a job as an assistant director. His most important new professional relationship was with Margit Gáspár (1905–94),[109] a communist intellectual appointed to manage three municipalised theatres. She made Karády a stage director and head of public relations at Városi Színház, the largest theatre in the city. Karády joined the communist party in April 1947, presumably because it was required for his new position. When Gáspár took over the Operetta Theatre in 1949, she invited Karády to join her. Karády's girlfriend was a soubrette at the Operetta, and if Karády took a high-level position there, it would have meant a conflict of interest. As he recalled,

> So I said, she shall go to the Operetta and … we create FŐNI. It happened that Margit Gáspár was on the committee … that divided theatres and actors [among themselves]. … I asked, 'So what happened to this person and that person?' 'Nothing. Wasn't even mentioned.' 'Well, if that's the case, let's make something out of this.' … Warm water was available in houses with central heating once a week. So we gathered on those days … in our house it was on Friday, in (János) Kublin's house on Tuesday … and there we had baths. One of us was in the bathtub, the other sitting on the toilet, the third … FŐNI was born there.[110]

Several reasons existed for establishing FŐNI. Under the state-socialist system, the only legal way of performing was as a member of a company – FŐNI provided job opportunities for actors. Perhaps the most significant reason, though, was Karády's own ambition. When Gáspár took over the Operetta Theatre, Karády contacted his superior, Gábor Goda, the cultural councillor on the Municipal Council, to ask if the Royal was going 'to be public property or left private'.[111] Karády had mastered the rhetoric of the Stalinist system and seeing the example of Gáspár, recognised an opportunity for himself.

Karády did not do this alone. He recruited friends and associates, none of whom had much professional theatre experience. For example, his friend János Kublin (1921–2001) was working for a film distribution company when the departing financial director of the Városi Színház recommended him as his replacement.[112] Kublin became the financial manager for FŐNI and brought his former classmate Egon Lázár (1921–2013) on board as an advisor.[113] Lázár recalled,

---

[109] Margit Gáspár was a writer and manager of the Operetta Theatre from 1949 to 1957.
[110] Conversation with Béla Karády, 26 September 2013.
[111] Letter from Béla Karády Béla to Gábor Goda, Municipal Advisor, 1 March 1949, KGY Varieté '66.
[112] According to Lázár, he was a theatrical goods buyer for Magyar Színház (Hungarian Theatre). Gáspár liked him so much that she took him with her to Városi Színház. Conversation with Egon Lázár, 7 June 2015.
[113] Because Lázár was Jewish, he had been forced to abandon his university studies and ordered into labour service. He fell captive to the Soviets in 194 and returned to Budapest in 1947, completely disillusioned with his religion.

Kublin knew ... nothing about financial leadership; he had a good sense of things but no knowledge. And I was home following imprisonment and he knew that I was working as ... an officer sending out past due notices at the Európa Publishing House. ... Kublin was in deep [distress] at the theatre and said to me, 'You're a bookkeeper. Come help me; you will be my acting manager.' Fine. Why, if I could be a doctor and a reinforced concrete engineer for the Russians, why can't I be a bookkeeper?[114]

The fourth member of FŐNI's leadership cadre was András Sólyom (1924–2012). Sólyom had organised occasional performances at the Városi Színház, where Karády befriended and subsequently employed him. Regarding his role in the company, Sólyom was referred to as the *shammes*[115] of Karády and Kublin (see Figure 7).

The production side of the FŐNI team was recruited from another circle of Karády's friends: established theatre professionals for whom the new system did not offer any work. Among them was Ernő Szabolcs, the sixty-two-year-old

Figure 7 The FŐNI's management on holiday at Lake Balaton, ca. 1950. Back row (l–r): András Sólyom, János Kublin, András Erős. Front row: Juci Hódossy (actor, Karády's girlfriend), Béla Karády, Mária Medveczky (Kublin's wife) and Mrs Erős. Egon Lázár, who took the photo, is not included.

---

[114] Conversation with Egon Lázár, 7 June 2015.
[115] Borrowed from the Yiddish שמשׁ, an official acting as the beadle, sexton and caretaker of a synagogue.

co-director of the 1925 show *Halló, Amerika!* The now doyen of operetta directors was subordinated to the twenty-seven-year-old newcomer Karády. Karády knew Imre Vogel, designer at the former Moulin Rouge, from the Royal and invited him to be part of FŐNI. Through Vogel, operetta composer Szabolcs Fényes joined the cadre. Even though Fényes was *persona non grata* (he was manager of the Operetta Theatre until 1949), Goda recognised his former tennis partner and offered him the position of FŐNI's musical director.[116]

Karády and his friends knew that they had to be acknowledged by the Party, but none of them had the personal prestige to make this happen. Furthermore, they had gathered around them discards from the private system, which did not help. Karády recalled,

> We needed the first man, one who maintains a good relationship with the Party. That's how (Endre) Székely came into the picture. ... Even though I was a Party member, I did not have a good relationship with the Party and neither did Kublin. His brother recently emigrated to Switzerland, and I ... [was told] that a communist cannot live in concubinage; so we needed someone acceptable for the Party and this is ... where 'Csúcsos' (Tapered) came from. ... The fact that he was a composer was a plus.[117]

'Tapered' was the nickname of composer Endre Székely (1912–39), who became the official general manager of FŐNI on the recommendation of Gáspár and her best friend, the sister of the Minister for People's Education. Székely's position was only titular, however: Karády and Kublin led FŐNI. After taking the job, Székely almost immediately left for a five-month ideological course and hardly involved himself in FŐNI affairs.[118]

The cadre was able to commandeer a major part of the entertainment sector thanks to personal relationships, professional networks and political alignments. Before 1945, neither Karády nor any of his friends could have managed a single theatre due to a lack of capital. Their limited professional experience would have made them ineligible for any leadership position. But because of the aggressive political transformation of cultural life, Karády, at age 27, was leading five theatres at the same time.

The main reason FŐNI could exist was that the political leadership did not have any plans for stage entertainment. This very mixed, low-prestige form of popular entertainment did not pose any threat to prominent theatre makers. The new enterprise was a low-level initiative in the sense that the Party leadership did not mandate its existence and that it did not copy an existing Soviet

---

[116] Sugár (1987: 48). [117] Conversation with Béla Karády, 27 October 2014.
[118] Székely did not mention FŐNI at all in a major interview about his life and career. Varga (1989: 9–17). He composed the first Hungarian socialist operetta, *Aranycsillag* (Golden Star), in 1950.

institution or structure, something that was expected in every field, whether it made sense or not. The Stalinist state accepted what Karády and his friends proposed since they had the support of people like Gábor Goda and Margit Gáspár.

On 8 October 1949, the police withdrew the licences of Royal Revü Varieté and Kamara Varieté and gave them to the Municipal Council, after which they became part of FŐNI. Karády recalled,

> My *Liebling* was the Royal Revue Theatre ... [my girlfriend] performed a couple of times under Teddy Ehrenthal ... so I knew my way around there. ... We had to nationalise. The process was that the state sent an excise officer [to each theatre] with a paper explaining what was happening. So each of us took this paper to a different place. I went to the Royal. We knocked on the door ... [and] handed Teddy Ehrenthal the paper about us nationalising the theatre. We had two things to ask for: the key to the safe and the keys to the car. He had a black Mercedes. ... He gave us [the keys] without a word. So the nationalisation was done.[119]

Ehrenthal, who acquired the theatre's management from the Soviets, feeling political pressure, did not attempt to resist. He performed the ritual of self-criticism and used communist speech patterns to express his loyalty to the State (see Figures 8 and 9). He tried to negotiate with authorities to keep the

Figure 8 Teddy Ehrenthal in 1945. *Színház*, 14 November 1945, p. 15.

---

[119] Conversation with Béla Karády, 26 September 2013.

Figure 9 Teddy Ehrenthal in 1949. *BÚÉK 1949*, p. 3.

management of the Moulin Rouge but did not succeed.[120] When he lost the Royal, he complained to the Municipal Council, but they did not even find his letter 'worthy of reflection'.[121] Ehrenthal was only a placeholder; nobody dealt with him long-term. What happened to him before his death in 1958 remains unknown.

On 15 October 1949, all the remaining privately managed entertainment venues in Budapest were subordinated to FŐNI. The company was responsible for a wide range of genres from opera (in Városi Színhaz) to circus shows in five venues and two open-air stages.

The transformation of the entertainment sphere also brought about changes in terminology. Such an attempt was not without precedent; for example, in December 1941, dance hosts employed by the clubs (*parkett-táncos*) were renamed *körtáncos* (round dancers). A decade later, while *varieté* and *revü* were already fluid terms, along with others like *vegyesműsor* (mixed show), which all described the same thing, a new one was quietly being introduced: *esztrád*. While *revü* was discarded on political grounds, *esztrád* was a safe word in the sense that it was borrowed from Russian and became increasingly accepted after the Театр Эстрады (Estrada Theatre) opened in Moscow in 1954.[122] Since

---

[120] Letter from Teddy Ehrenthal to the Bureau of Soviet Assets in Hungary, 23 April 1949, BFL XIV. 265. 3. d.

[121] Memorandum to Mr István Ehrenthal, 8 October 1949, KGY Feljegyzések Szőnyi-ügyben.

[122] György Szépe, a linguist at the Institute of Linguistic Studies, claimed that 'esztrád is not a necessary word by any means' and did not recommend using it. Kérdezz-felelek. *Élet és Tudomány*, 6 June 1956, p. 716.

the image of showgirls was the polar opposite of new images of the working woman and mother, the word *görl* disappeared from public discourse for the next ten to fifteen years, although it still appeared in internal documents.

3.3 Show Business in the State-Socialist Theatre System

In 1950, a new state theatre structure was established on the Soviet model.[123] Ilus Vay, a comic actress, described the differences between the two systems:

> Previously, a theatre was managed by three people: the manager, the secretary and a (female) secretary who did the administration, calculated and paid wages, distributed tickets and before she let issues go to the management, personally filtered and evaluated them. Now suddenly a party secretary was necessary, along with a trade union deputy, an arranger of membership stamps and other very important persons under God knows what titles.[124]

The primary task of the management and the creative team was now to serve the political interests of their superiors. If they did not comply, they were quickly let go. Such demands appeared in every segment of cultural life.[125] The most successful theatre leaders of the period (Tamás Major at the National Theatre and Margit Gáspár at the Operetta Theatre) could sometimes resist the mandates through their political prestige, but they were exceptions.

The state theatre system meant that the Ministry of People's Education now determined the number and profile of theatres.[126] The Minister directly appointed the theatre managers, who with resident dramaturgs, planned their seasons, which then had to be submitted to and approved by the Theatre Department of the Ministry. The manager had the right to select his creative team and artists; however, matters of hiring and firing also had to be approved by the Ministry. Artists could only be contracted for an entire season; if a role could not be cast in-house, the management could hire someone from another theatre, but only with the Ministry's approval. Each manager had to hold weekly staff meetings and send minutes to the Ministry.

FŐNI theatres were reorganised according to this new structure, though many of the new positions did not make sense with their types of offerings. Positions such as dramaturg, writer or even director were not sharply defined (or even existed!) in the entertainment sphere before 1949. So much so that Vilmos Tarján, a gossip columnist – and manager of the Royal Orfeum from 1924 to 1926 – joked about it earlier:

---

[123] Nyáry (1950: 6).
[124] Vay (2006: 153). The Royal had 113 employees, which would have been inconceivable for a private theatre. This number increased to 164 in 1951. Minute book of the session of the Municipal Council, 13 July 1951, BFL XXIII. 102. a. 1. p. 72.
[125] Gyarmati (2021: 122–130).   [126] Heltai (2011a: 112–117); cf. Korossy (2007).

> A guest asked me: Who is that gentleman?
> – He's the dramaturg of the Papagáj (Club).
> – Why does the Papagáj need a dramaturg?
> – To select the women.[127]

In many ways, FŐNI was unique. While theoretically every theatre was equal and had the same cultural (political) worth, this was far from reality. The sharp distinction between venues geared toward entertainment and those that were not, remained and in fact widened. FŐNI was not a member of the new professional organisation, Magyar Színház- és Filmművészeti Szövetség (Hungarian Theatre- and Film Association), and the Ministry did nothing to help change this.[128] Twice the Ministry gave bonuses to the employees of state theatres, but not to those of FŐNI. FŐNI was the only company to control multiple theatres; the rest reported individually to the Ministry of People's Education. Unlike those theatres, FŐNI was profit oriented. Its unified budget allowed for some financial flexibility within the structure. When they were under the private system, managers of FŐNI theatres had control over choosing productions and performers, now their roles were merely administrative. Every significant decision was made or ratified by FŐNI's Central Management – Karády and Kublin.[129] The two of them intended to keep as much power as possible to themselves and make their theatre managers *de facto* secretaries. As Karády recalled,

> I decided that Tom, Dick and Harry will perform in the show, but the contract was written and negotiated by the ... theatre manager. [It] became valid only when the Central Management – namely me – signed it. ... I think it was clear that the Central Management had the power, and they only did minor tasks.[130]

The collapse of this new system was only a matter of time. In fact, Karády and Kublin were only able to keep their positions for one season. By June 1950, FŐNI had become entangled in a complex web of conflicts, and its position was weakened both externally and internally.[131] On one hand, managers were trying to become more independent and secure actual managerial rights for themselves. On the other, the attitude of the Municipal Council had changed. Gábor Goda, the 'patron' of FŐNI, resigned to focus on his new career as a novelist. His successor had a radically different opinion on how shows were supposed to

---

[127] Tarján (1940: 49).
[128] Letter from Antal Berzeller to the XI. Dept. of the Municipal Council, 18 February 1950, BFL XXIII. 114. 4. d.
[129] The salary and employment of performers were determined by the Ministry of People's Education and seat prices by the Municipal Council. Letter from Pál Hámos and János Kublin to the theatre department of the Ministry of People's Education, 29 December 1949, BFL XXIII. 114. 4. d.
[130] Conversation with Béla Karády, 26 September 2013.   [131] Molnár (2019a: 133–157).

look. The result of this two-front war was that Karády and his colleagues were officially sacked at the season-closing company meeting on 22 June 1950.[132]

FŐNI, though, continued. A certain Mrs Sásdi,[133] a cleaning lady at the Grand Hotel, was named general manager. This was in line with the impractical ideological practice of appointing physical workers to lead state companies. Many of these 'worker managers' never had been in an actual factory or business, and they often knew nothing about the profession they were supposed to lead.[134] Mrs Sásdi fit this profile, for she was ignorant about theatre. Though she and her new management team were not going to be attacked politically, they had a major problem: performers and other artists were resisting the new aggressively politicised leadership style. This led to contradictory instructions and increasingly unclear job expectations. Within a few months, the artistic work had become extremely chaotic, which resulted in a widespread institutional crisis.

The weekly meetings of almost every sector of the Municipal Music Hall were devoted to complaining. The orchestra straight-out criticised the leadership for ignoring the fundamental aspects of putting on a show: '[The composer] Szabolcs Fényes is not involved in pre-production, even though the basis of the revue is the music. There are two directors, but there is still no finale as of today. ... The audience only notices that the show is over when the orchestra leaves'.[135] Then, at an actors' meeting, Gertrúd Romváry pointed out the political pressure and the demoralising atmosphere:

> [She] asked many times: Who is the artistic director here? Who is the manager? There are eight directors here, and staging instructions come in the form of orders, not like they are discussed with the actor. What kind of order is this, she once asked. An order from above, she was told, so she cannot criticise it because it comes from above her.[136]

News of these problems reached the Ministry by spring 1951, for in April of that year FŐNI was disbanded. Only two years after the theatre industry's municipalisation–nationalisation, its operations had to be revised. FŐNI venues remained in municipal ownership, but now as independent theatres.

---

[132] Minute book of the company session in the Municipal Music Hall, 22 June 1950, BFL XXXV. 103. c. 535. ő. e.

[133] Her full maiden name and other details of her life are unknown. She was referred in internal documents only as Mrs Sásdi.

[134] Mihályi (2018: 23).

[135] Minute book of the orchestra's production meeting of the Municipal Music Hall, 21 April 1951, BFL VIII. 3806. 8. d.

[136] Minute book of the actors' production meeting of the Municipal Music Hall, 20 April 1951, BFL VIII. 3806. 8. d.

At the Municipal Music Hall, the Ministry of People's Education appointed István Fejér as manager. Fejér, a former journalist for the weekly theatre magazine *Színház és Mozi* (Theatre and Cinema), rebranded the theatre as Fővárosi Víg Színház (Municipal Gaiety Theatre) and began a Ministry-approved experiment with revues. The venture failed, and after just one season, the theatre changed its focus to operettas.

Public demand for a music hall (even if it didn't offer revues) was such that plans for a new venue were announced in May 1952. The former Kamara Cinema, built on the site of a hotel swimming pool in the city centre, was to be refurbished for this purpose. The new venue was to be called Fővárosi Nagy Varieté (Municipal Grand Music Hall), even though it was smaller than the Royal. While the Royal was being renovated to mount operettas, the building's condition was discovered to be so bad that it could not be saved, and it was demolished in 1953. So, rather than the Fővárosi Nagy Varieté, the Fővárosi Víg Színház moved into the former cinema, and, yet again, operetta superseded music hall.

The second reorganisation of state theatres within five years took place in 1954. The Fővárosi Víg Színház lost its independence and was subordinated to the Operetta Theatre.[137] Since Fővárosi Nagy Varieté did not materialise, the Országos Cirkusz Vállalat (National Circus Company), opened the small Budapest Varieté (Budapest Music Hall) on the edge of the VIII district, far from the historical theatre district. Béla Karády was its first manager, who intended to create a 'small Royal'; but its budget and infrastructure made it impractical for revues, and it closed in 1960.

3.4 Nationalising Nightlife

The nationalisation of clubs and the catering trade happened in waves similar to that of the theatres. Between 21 and 31 January 1949, thirty-eight bars and coffee houses were nationalised, fourteen of which immediately closed. In some cases, drastic design changes were made, such as the removal of the chinoiserie interior at the former Sanghay Club. By the end of the year, another ninety-one venues had been nationalised and subordinated to the newly created Éttermi és Büfé Vállalat (Restaurant and Buffet Company). The process was quick, as an anonymous former employee recalled:

> The owner did not come in for the second day in a row. We knew that he had been well-informed through his connections. . . . It was around 5 p.m. when we heard that the nationalising committee [was coming]. By that time nobody was working; the guests were sent away . . . only a curious couple remained. Three of us were sitting in the office, the cashier, the bookkeeper and me, who

---

[137] Sugár (1987: 50). For an analysis of its final season and the political context, see Heltai (2013).

was in charge of the finances. ... As 'the boss's men', we were quite concerned. Three men came up – they were at least as anxious as we were – two of them from the trade union and the third who we recognised as the head waiter from the Abbázia [a coffee house]. 'We are nationalising the shop in the name of the people', said one of them. ... They reported on the act of nationalisation, collected money and valuables from the cash desk, regardless of where they came from, what they were for or who owned them, and handed them to the appointed company leader. ... One of the trade union members vigorously warned us: 'From this moment, the former owner is not allowed to enter. Everything here has been seized in the name of the people, for he obtained this [capital] through the exploitation of workers. None of you should attempt to give him or smuggle out any items, objects or valuables because we will punish such actions according to the law. For now, you can continue working and then we'll see'.[138]

Starting in 1951, control was decentralised and district companies managed the venues. The secret police kept a close eye on the Moulin Rouge and other clubs.[139] Foreigners were regulars at these places because their offerings were more accessible to them than the experimental revues, which were mainly in Hungarian. (Also, diplomatic immunity meant security from the police.) Several Hungarian actresses found foreign suitors in the bars; the State secret police attempted to recruit these women and have them report on their boyfriends. Refusing the 'offer' had serious consequences, such as being banned from the stage and family members losing their jobs. Those who accepted were rewarded.[140]

Controlling the content of performances in the clubs and coffee houses became another problem. Before 1949, such shows were organised by the management or through agents. After 1949, private individuals were forbidden to produce anything on stage.[141] Clubs depended on their clientele and to keep them, they sometimes ignored what was happening on stage. As one observer noted, 'Most of the hostile remarks were not in the written text but in the (improvised) jokes of the actors, against which the manager of the venue did not do anything but was happy that there were two more laughs and that a certain part of the audience was enjoying itself'.[142]

In 1953, the Municipal Council established the Budapest Műsoriroda (Budapest Production Office) to better control the club shows and their musicians. Soon it was

---

[138] Zsiray (1969: 3–4).   [139] See Havadi (2008).
[140] For the story of Ida Boros, whose theatre career was supported by the secret police in exchange for her reports, see Molnár (2019a: 183–193), and her secret police folder ÁBTL B-81836.
[141] Desperate artists still found loopholes. A family act called Halálkatlan (Death Cauldron) performed in front of the Western Railway Station, and the Ministry had to investigate how that could happen. Gusztáv Erdős' letter to György Heitz, 19 November 1953, MNL OL XIX-I-3-a 363. d.
[142] Minute book of the Municipal Council meeting, 8 January 1953, BFL XXIII.102.a.1 p. 29.

reorganised as Népi- és Tánczenei Központ (Folk and Dance Music Centre) but managers complained that this centralised system was ineffective and expensive. Every musical programme had to be submitted to this body. Some Western European songs performed with Hungarian lyrics were generally included, though it was advised to have no more than two or three such songs out of a total of eight-to-ten pieces. Informants went from club to club, noting who played what.[143]

Following a successful lobby after the 1956 Revolution, clubs were able to hire their own artists. The Moulin Rouge, renamed Budapest Kávéház (Budapest Coffee House), was the only major nightclub of the previous era to still produce shows, though hardly any information about them survives. Dance and musical acts dominated (one of the best bands in town was still playing there), and significantly fewer artists appeared on its stage than previously. Protectionism kept this number small.[144] Since the system of control was not prepared to handle non-theatrical productions, clubs maintained a bit of autonomy. These productions were not part of the socialist revue experiments; they were barely acknowledged and only rarely advertised in the papers.

4 The Socialist Revue Experiments

Even though revues were largely ignored under the new theatre system, the genre remained popular. Revues had to be legitimised in the new cultural context, which valued only their 'educative' features. Therefore, an approach to the genre needed to be found or created that would satisfy both politicians and audiences. Although entertainment was already nationalised once during the brief Soviet Republic of Hungary in 1919[145] and the Hungarian worker's theatre movement in the 1930s produced leftist political shows, none of these precedents were known by those now in charge.[146]

4.1 The Trade Union's Alternative to Private Entertainment

The first revue experiment happened before the municipalisation of theatres. In June 1949, the Trade Union sponsored and produced a revue on the open-air stage at *Angol Park* (Amusement Park). Written by István Fejér, a journalist

---

[143] Péter Agonás: Nekrológ az Argényi zenekarról; cited in Simon (1999: 135).

[144] 'Thanks to (Rudolf) Halász (lyricist and cabaret author) and his manipulations, there is an unbreakable clique of female performers in several catering venues; the same people perform for years, because either financially or in 'other' ways they secured their positions'. Anonymous report, n. d. (1953?), MNL OL XIX-I-3-a 363. d.

[145] Orpheums were to be 'radically reformed', but not the genre itself. See Lukács György a kommunizált színházak jövőjéről. *Színházi Élet*, 30 March 1919.

[146] See the bequest of László Balogh PIL VI. 935. f. 13. ő. e.

who was perhaps the loudest voice against private entertainment, *Meserevű* (Fairy Tale Revue) reflected his personal dictates. According to Fejér, a revue should be

> written by writers who don't see expressing the optimistic, cheerful message of the era as a burden. ... [The revue] should not be a pulpit for political theorems ... nor the messenger of the world view of the grand bourgeoisie. ... It should be witty and fun and not merge humour with obscenity. At the same time, it should not be any less spectacular than the old revue. ... It should not be written around the 'star' ... the artist should serve the revue.[147]

While the show's book is lost, its overall plan is known: contrasting scenes depicting the 'old times' and the 'present' were alternated to convey the superiority of the present. Fejér reviewed his own show in a theatre magazine and chastised the production team for ignoring and removing its political messages.[148] Three months later, FŐNI was established, and Fejér's experiments with revues ended.

4.2 FŐNI Revues

Creating ideological content for revues was not a priority of the FŐNI management – they were busy enough managing and staging new productions. Nevertheless, as the number of political attacks grew, Karády responded with a thirty-page document. He was heavily influenced by the strategy of his mentor Gáspár, who was in the process of legitimising operetta under the new system. Her strategy was to create a new origin story for operetta that would allow the genre 'to be reformed'. This new narrative has been thoroughly analysed by Gyöngyi Heltai, who uses Eric Hobsbawm's term 'invented tradition' for what was happening.[149] The key components of Gáspár's strategy were:

- To discredit the legacy of the genre using 'scientific' arguments.
- To adopt an educative tone with seemingly new thoughts, without providing any supporting sources.
- To defer to the political leadership's absolute right to influence the form and content of stage entertainment.
- To describe the development of the genre through dialectic materialism, placing it among the struggles between 'good' and 'evil'.

---

[147] István Fejér: Miért rossz a régi revű? Milyen legyen az új? *Színház és Mozi*, 11 May 1949, p. 24.
[148] István Fejér: Kritikus kritikája saját darabjáról. *Színház és Mozi*, 8 June 1949, p. 5.
[149] See Gáspár (1949) and Heltai (2012: 50).

- To demonstrate how the appearance of capitalism 'corrupted' the genre, which must be reformed according to the Soviet example to find its 'right path' again.

Karády included all these arguments in his own essay. He established the origins of institutionalised light entertainment in the Stone Age (!), claiming that its history had been compromised, even criminalised, by capitalism. He asserted that the disgraced capitalist past cannot be seen as an obstacle in reforming the genre, for the works produced then were not even proper revues. He claimed that new revues should:

- Discard obscenity and emphasise humour.
- Aim for a middle course between entertainment and political propaganda – it is acceptable to make the acts propagandistic but it should not be obligatory.
- Have a frame story or a specific theme, but this should not dominate the revue.
- Increase the role of writers.[150]

4.2.1 The Productions

Between 1949 and 1951, FŐNI produced seven original revues at the Municipal Music Hall. These revues were not adaptations, reworkings or revivals. Neither were they based on Soviet models.[151] Hungarian papers occasionally reported on Soviet-modelled circuses and similar offerings, but entertainment was not considered politically important enough (unlike agriculture, for instance) that a trip to the Soviet Union could have been arranged for the people in charge.

FŐNI's creative team, under its Central Management, prepared every production and no individual writers were named in printed materials: 'the writing community of the Municipal Music Hall' was credited as the author. (A couple of months earlier, the first production of the state Operetta Theatre had listed its creators the same way.) This expression suggested equality among the creative team, though political influence from above was certainly present. Before 1949, the 'text' was compiled from the jokes of the performers and developed from rehearsal to rehearsal or even performance to performance. In the socialist revues, a fixed text became essential because it was easy to control. Censorship generally focused on the libretto and improvisation was strictly forbidden. Even after a full year, seasoned writers were still unsure of what was

---

[150] The development of entertainment. n. d., KGY Varieté '66, p. 31.

[151] This was easier for the Operetta Theatre, although the adaptation of Soviet operettas sometimes necessitated a complete rewrite. In the case of Shcherbachov's *Табачный капитан* (Tobacco Captain), it also meant recomposing the music. See Heltai (2012: 161).

allowed or not allowed. As Dezső Kellér noted, 'Writers need hints. We have to write about male–female relationships; there is and there will be love. What about blue stories, are they allowed within tasteful borders or not?'[152]

The first two productions under the new management, *Botrány az Állatkertben* (Scandal in the Zoo, October 1949) and *Új világ csillagai* (Stars of a New World, December 1949), consisted of chains of different acts, following pre-1949 practice. Artists had already been engaged before the change in protocol, and keeping the illusion of continuity was a political priority.[153] The content of these shows, however, was politicised, for example, in having showgirls advertise the newly established state department stores (see Figure 10).

Karády's ideal revue structure did not consist of independent scenes with different themes following one another but rather was centred around an overall theme or frame story into which different scenes or acts were inserted.[154] His approach not only provided more unity to the production but also was deemed

Figure 10 Showgirls advertising the opening of the Fiftieth State Department Store, 1949.

---

[152] Minute book of the FŐNI artistic meeting, 14 October 1950, BFL IV. 1521. 1. d.
[153] Letter from Endre Székely to the XI. Dept. of the Municipal Council, 16 September 1949, KGY FŐNI-ügy.
[154] These two approaches were also evident in revues that appeared on Broadway and in London's West End, with the latter (Karády's preference) being more prominent.

more acceptable from a political point of view, as it made transmitting a 'message' easier. It did not negate earlier formats per se, as revues existed in many different forms before 1949, but it did limit the possibilities of the genre. Since each individual act had to be logically inserted into the framing device, the challenge became how to create a plot either formed around the acts or told through the acts.

The most successful FŐNI revue was *Májusfa* (Maypole), which played in April 1950. Its overarching plot concerns a young textile worker who develops a new poplin that does not shrink after its first wash. He loses the shirt made from the sample fabric, which he has to find so he can present it to the factory manager. The hunt through the streets of Budapest provides the frame for the different acts. Before 1949, it would have been the female lead who was the main feature of the production; now, it was a working *bon vivant*, a young hero whose positive actions embodied the socialist utopia. The second most important role was that of the likeminded *soubrette*. In the course of the revue, these principal characters find each other and true happiness in the utopistic social context. Neither has a private sphere or life away from the public eye and politics: they represent new types of ideal citizens. The plot is enhanced through supporting stock characters, who by the end of the revue have discarded their earlier values and behaviours and have adopted the new ones represented by the heroes. Such characters were played by established comedians like Kálmán Latabár or Alfonzó. Their roles were personalised, which could mean that their reputations were being exploited politically as well as allowing the continuation of certain performance styles. (Traditional comedians were not compatible with socialist stock characters, though they remained popular.) Other stock characters represented a reactionist type based on propagandistic images of the 'enemy of the state'. They were either the villains, who represented the old world and did everything in their power to sabotage the new order, or characters whose Western tastes and style of dress were played for mockery.

The Association of Theatre Arts played a significant role in how cultural products, including revues, were perceived. It organised conferences and public forums for the discussion of theoretical questions and artistic policies. Such debates were seen as vital political tools at the time, for they provided spaces for political (self-)criticism.[155] During a discussion of *Májusfa*, for example, one participant complained about the characters' collective lack of depth in the revue, since dance and different acts still dominated the show. The conclusion, though, when it came to promoting socialist messages, was that 'the revue could be as much a weapon in our hands as any other genre'.[156]

---

[155] For more on this, see Korossy (2007: 114–120).
[156] Comment of Imre Apáthy, Minute book of the discussion of *Májusfa* at the Association of Theatre Arts, 13 May 1950, KGY Májusfa-vita.

The legitimacy of the revue did not matter to FŐNI's 'cleaning-lady' management team. Because they weren't theatre professionals, they could not understand the nature of the experiments and the fact that this type of theatre could not work according to the dictates of socialist realism. They kept complaining about the 'lack of plays', and while Karády was aiming to balance political messages with entertainment, the productions that appeared after he left became extremely propagandistic. In *Jó reggelt Budapest!* (Good Morning Budapest!, 1951), for example, the villain was the son of a mill owner with German roots who Hungarianised his name. He tried to steal the first Hungarian cotton seeds from the hero's girlfriend, as well as the girlfriend. The finale suggested that he was beaten to death offstage in an act of vigilantism by the hero's friend.

Dance scenes and specialty acts remained important in these shows. The percentage of stage time devoted to them, however, significantly dropped while that for dialogue and the spoken word increased. Acts were often in styles that traditionally belonged to elite culture (such as classical music, ballet etc.) and therefore served as a tool of legitimation. Only one or two such acts remained in the productions on average, since writers had to create logical, diegetic occasions to feature them, and they had to appear realistic (see Figure 11). In earlier revues, children were hardly ever featured; however, FŐNI revues now included complete children's choruses. Some scenes were even cast with kindergarten kids playing stock socialist characters, just like the adults. Although animal acts were part of the earlier revue tradition, they rarely appeared in FŐNI revues. On one hand, it was particularly challenging to send political messages through such acts; on the other, characters could not go to the circus in every show.

Finding a politically acceptable frame story posed a massive challenge for the creators. One strategy was to announce a public competition, hoping that they could find somebody capable of writing a proper propaganda piece. Every genre that was having problems reconciling ideology and format tried this approach; there were even several competitions to write clown jokes for the circus. Although the cash prizes were very large (the first prize was 5,000 Forints and the second 3,000, when the monthly per capita income did not reach 500 Forints for a quarter of working-class families),[157] nothing useful ever arrived. So, creators had to keep coming up with their own ideas.

4.2.2 Casting

Another challenge concerned choosing performers. When FŐNI was established in autumn 1949, new managers at the state theatres were appointed, and actors who were deemed politically eligible were hired. Remarks

---
[157] Romsics (1999: 280).

Figure 11 '2 Argos' acrobats in *Jó reggelt, Budapest!*

concerning several actors survive in Karády's personal archive (see Table 1). These include comments not only on their talent but also on their demeanour and political leanings.

The company system provided security for the performers who were selected, though they were permanently assigned to a specific theatre. Those not offered positions were now completely excluded from what had been their professional livelihood. For instance, the operetta legend Sári Fedák was banned from the stage until her death in 1955. Some performers were assigned to provincial theatres, which was seen as a form of punishment since anything outside the capital was regarded by default as professionally inferior.

Table 1 Remarks on performers being considered for the Municipal Entertainment Company (excerpt)

Name[a]	Handwritten Remarks
Sándor Szabó György Gozmány	both assigned to Miskolc, on Monday arrange it with Jákó not to be taken to the countryside
Erzsi Galambos	had a disciplinary hearing, not needed
Magda Gyenes	suspected fascist
Erzsi Rév	? the wife of Graumann but she actively participated in the resistance and a very nice person
Berta Türk	behaves well
Árpád Latabár	good
Ilus Vay	suspected arrow cross [party sympathiser]
Klári Vértes	excellent

[a]Attachment to the cadre proposal for the Municipal Entertainment Company, n. d., KGY Royal Revű Varieté.

Budapest theatre was sharply defined through a hierarchy of genres. A higher value was given to forms that interpreted a dramatic text and a significantly lower one to those that relied more on physicality. Ida Turay, a former star, remembered being assigned to a music hall:

> I was immediately 'deported' to the Kamara Varieté, you can imagine what a drop it was for me. I was dressing with an artist whose main act was that her body and hair sparkled. . . . I found it humiliating.[158]

Since Turay no longer had the types of roles she once did in the leading dramatic theatres of Budapest, she took every opportunity to avoid performing and had her understudy cover for her almost every evening.[159] The fact that Ida Turay, who left the country after the 1956 Revolution, or stars like Katalin Karády and Sári Déry were not offered contracts by a prestigious theatre carried a strong message: their star status and the character types they had played on stage and screen were both nullified.

As the Iron Curtain descended, the notions of foreign artists in Budapest and Hungarian artists abroad became politicised, including the process through which they were hired. Before 1949, a manager or agent would go abroad to

---

[158] Szántó (1985: 489). Turay refers to *Tótágas* (Upside down) at the Kamara Varieté in January 1950, in which such an act, Wolton's Electric Chair, appeared. Turay worked in music halls at the beginning of her career and thought she had moved beyond what she deemed lower venues. See Az új Royal Orfeum. *Esti Kurír*, 17 August 1926.

[159] See the stage manager's reports in BFL VIII. 3808. 1. d.

watch an act before offering a contract. After the borders were sealed, this was no longer possible and the only way to secure an international booking was through photos sent by post, which did not mean anything. So, FŐNI began lobbying to travel to other Soviet Bloc countries in search of talent, though without success. After 1950, no foreign artists were contracted for the music halls, and hardly any for the circus. The Kultúrkapcsolatok Intézete (Institute for Cultural Relations) was in charge of hiring from abroad, but the entertainment sphere was not among its priorities. The Hungarian market was too small to be self-sufficient. Access to the Western professional network was blocked, and building a new Eastern one did not happen quickly, despite the demand from other countries.[160] After a ministerial meeting in the autumn of 1951, a system of *artistacsere* (artist exchange) was developed, allowing Hungarian artists to work abroad. First, a professional committee ranked the artists, then the State Security checked them and the Ministry of People's Education sent them abroad as an official cultural deputy. Three acts travelled to Czechoslovakia in September 1952 as part of the scheme, which remained in place until the second half of the 1950s.

Soon after FŐNI was established, the question of education and training of new show business performers emerged – at least on a rhetorical level.[161] This aligned with the old professional demand of having a dedicated school.[162] Nevertheless, performers were expected to represent and serve socialist ideals replacing those who had been banned. The Theatre Academy ignored the demands of the entertainment sphere both before and after Sovietisation, and although FŐNI's in-house school failed, a State Ballet Institute and a State Circus Institute were established in 1950 to replace private schools and provide the necessary professional training.

The Hungarian Dance Association was established in 1948 to develop a 'socialist dance culture', but it focused on ensemble dancing, not stage dancing.[163] Three areas were created: folk dance, ballet and 'modern dance' (*mozdulatművészet* – movement art),[164] the last of which was soon eliminated. Several modern dancers ended up choreographing for the music hall, since this became their only option if they wanted to continue dancing. Tap, swing and *mondain* were banned from the stage, in favour of folk, ballet and national dances of the Eastern bloc. New 'socialist' dances, like the *Lipsi* in the German

---

[160] Czechoslovakia proposed an exchange already in 1949, and at the time Czechoslovak artists were working in other countries of the Bloc.
[161] Letter to the Mayor, n. d. (1949), KGY Feljegyzések Szőnyi-ügyben.
[162] Artista iskola. *Artisták Lapja*, 15 July 1920, p. 1.
[163] Constitution of the Hungarian Dance Associaton, n. d. (1948), OSZMI TA Bequest of Zsuzsa Ortutay 7. d. 201. 10. 44.
[164] See Fuchs-Füged. 2016.

Democratic Republic (DDR), were not developed in Hungary. Starting with the second FŐNI production, guest dancers from the Hungarian State Opera performed in the revues.

Before 1949, audiences were often introduced to new dance styles on the parquet of a nightclub or on the stage of a music hall. After 1949, this activity was politically reinterpreted at the Municipal Music Hall. One example occurs in a scene from *Májusfa*, set at a Saturday evening party, as Ria and Ödön, the stock comic reactionaries, arrive.

> (The orchestra begins playing a foxtrot; girls and boys are dancing. Ria and Ödön enter with a lot of luggage.)
> Ödön: ... Would you like to dance?
> Ria: Of course I would! At least we can show them what a real foxtrot is! Come! (They begin to dance, spinning and shaking the American way. The others, as they notice them, wave and poke each other, laughing. Slowly everyone stops; only Ria and Ödön are left dancing as they are drowned out with laughter. They bemusedly stop and greet those who have been watching.)
> Feri: I think you are a bit lost! This is not a crazy ball! (big laughter)[165]

The political goal here was to instruct the audience on the 'correct' way of dancing, as opposed to the 'crazy' idea of 'shaking the American way'. Nevertheless, the actual performers could have reinterpreted the stage directions, making it less of a mockery, especially if it was supported by the music. The foxtrot was followed by a polka, which led into the first finale and implied the polka's cultural importance and dominance over the foxtrot.

As for the chorus, twelve physically attractive young women were chosen in an open casting call. Comments on their auditions reflect the importance of their physical appearance, particular styles of dancing and sometimes other attributes (see Table 2).

Although the number of female dancers was less than before (in 1948, the Royal had fifteen, and in the 1930s the Moulin Rouge employed sixteen), earlier criteria, like being 'pretty', remained decisive. Kublin's name appearing next to that of Fabriczki could mean that she was simply his protégé but it also could mean that Karády was marking her as someone for him to hit on.

Twelve young men were engaged to form a male chorus to complement the female one. This notion was not entirely new: in 1929, twelve men were hired for *Miss Amerika*, though the intention there was not to create a counterpart to the forty-member female chorus.

After being hired to appear in a *FŐNI* production, keeping one's job required supporting the political ideology. Two dancers did not have their

---

[165] Májusfa-script, KGY Librettók.

Table 2 Comments made at dancers' audition (excerpt)

Name[a]	Comments
Mária Fabriczki	tap, ballet, very attractive pretty girl (Kublin)
Hédi Nemes	(ex-Royal girl) pretty, to the studio!!
Elli Faragó	perhaps teachable
Ibolya Tamás	(ex-artist, interesting, not a pretty face) excellent acrobat, learns any kind of dance, *komisch* (comic) too!!
Andrea Szerdahelyi	(seventeen years old) character and ballet
Bea Körössy	pretty (ex-Royal)

[a]Dance audition, n. d. (May 1950), KGY 1950.

contracts renewed because they were not 'sympathetic to building socialism'.[166] Morale among the chorus was understandably low: most of the 114 disciplinary cases that were heard between September 1950 and January 1951 concerned dancers' behaviour (e.g., being late for rehearsal).

4.3 The Municipal Gaiety Theatre Revues

After FŐNI's liquidation, the Municipal Council and the Ministry of People's Education appointed István Fejér as manager of the Municipal Music Hall, which he and director György Rácz renamed Fővárosi Víg Színház (Municipal Gaiety Theatre). Fejér, who had already experimented with revues in 1949, and Rácz wanted to start from scratch as far as what they would present at the theatre. This was one reason they renamed the venue: they wanted to give it a 'higher' cultural rank. They discarded previous experiments with revues and even the word *revü*, instead calling their productions *zenés-táncos vidám játék* (a merry musical play with dancing).

The theatre remained under the budget of the Municipality, but Fejér kept a close connection with the Ministry of People's Education. Political response now had to be considered during the creative process, which extended the time it took to create a new show.[167] Hence, only three shows were produced in the 1951–52 season. One month after the Municipal Gaiety Theatre opened, Mihály

---

[166] Monthly report about the work of the Municipal Music Hall, 29 December 1950, BFL IV. 1521. 18. d.

[167] '[T]wo weeks before opening night we have finished rehearsals of our new piece, so we have time to incorporate the corrections from the notes of the Public Education Department. Their comments on the text of our piece were thoroughly evaluated, discussed and answered'. Monthly report about the work of the Municipal Gaiety Theatre, 29 April 1952, BFL VII. 3806. 7. d.

Farkas, Minister of Homeland Defence, attended a performance. As part of Rákosi's inner circle, his appreciation of what he experienced meant political support for the management's creative approach.[168]

The principles of Fejér and Rácz were similar to those behind the previous socialist revue experiments. One major difference, though, was their demand for naturalism and 'reflecting reality'.[169] For them, the revue was not the acts or the large-scale scenes but rather the text. Revues required a plot into which individual acts and visually spectacular scenes could be organically inserted and through which Rácz, as director, could communicate the 'message' of the authors. Nonetheless, six months and two staged revues later, he changed his opinion, asserting that 'The revue is the only theatre genre whose main master is not the writer but the director'.[170]

Through such remarks, Rácz was legitimising what he was doing in actual practice. The role of the stars was further reduced; in fact, no big names appeared in the last two shows. Villains were eliminated as characters. On one hand, this made it more difficult to create plots, while on the other, the productions gained a lighter tone. Because Rácz's shows were text-based and plot-driven, they were not that different from operettas. Still, Rácz, following cultural policy, argued that his productions should be sharply distinguished from other genres.[171]

As for the performing style, the Stanislavski method (or at least the managers' understanding of it) was forced on the actors at the Municipal Gaiety Theatre, as it was at every theatre in Hungary. It did not matter that a psycho-realist approach made no sense for this genre. Rózsi Csikós, a soubrette, noted: '[W]e have heard the word *psychophysical* several times, but so far it has not managed to inspire interest. I agree with the directive that we should learn what it means in practice'.[172] The Stanislavski technique could not work for socialist-realist stock characters, nor for roles built around a performer's image and personality. 'Going deep' was impossible and pointless for minor characters that only had a few lines. The comedian Alfonzó struggled with this requirement: 'I wait fifteen

---

[168] The management had to ask the Ministry for permission to try a different dramaturgy for their third show. Monthly report about the work of the Municipal Gaiety Theatre, 26 February 1952, BFL VIII. 3806. 7. d. During his dictatorship, Rákosi only visited the Operetta Theatre, never the music halls.

[169] Three-month production plan of the Municipal Gaiety Theatre, 11 October 1951, BFL VIII. 3806. 7. d.

[170] Minute book of the conference *Kell-e revü és ha igen, milyen legyen?*, 17 February 1952, OSZK SzT Fond 16/4.

[171] 'we would like to distinguish ourselves from dramatic genres and related musical genres but from the tempting sidepaths of variety shows and estrada'. Minute book of the conference *Kell-e revü és ha igen, milyen legyen?*, 17 February 1952, OSZK SzT Fond 16/4.

[172] Minute book of the Stanilslavski-club session, 1 March 1952, BFL VIII. 3806. FVSZ 9. d.

minutes for my entrance during which I play a bit with the monkey, trying to imagine somehow that I am a zookeeper'.[173]

The first production at the Municipal Gaiety Theatre was a heavily revised version of a Hungarian literary classic from 1790, *A peleskei nótárius* (The Scrivener from Peleske). The source material was familiar to the audience, as it had been adapted for the stage and revived many times. This new version (whose libretto is lost) places socialist-realist stock characters and situations drawn from a vulgar Marxist interpretation of history into the eighteenth-century setting. For instance, ordinary bridge builders help the heroic scrivener escape from the police.

The plot of the second production, *Címe: ismeretlen* (Recipient: Unknown), offered a search narrative, as did *Májusfa*. A lieutenant from the countryside is trying to find the girl in Budapest who, in his absence, saved his mother's life by donating blood for a transfusion. Despite its peculiar premise, the revue was very successful and played 141 performances. Fejér and his associates were at a loss as to what to do next. At the professional preview of *Címe: ismeretlen* on 9 January 1952, he expressed his concerns about the socialist revue being allowed only one dramaturgical approach: '[I]n our theatre we are the only ones who frankly and honestly admit that we would like to experiment. We were commissioned personally by comrade Révai (Minister of People's Education) to create the socialist revue [but] we don't know what the job is, and what the result should look like. We are poking about for it, poking'.[174]

For the third revue, *Most jelent meg* (The Latest Issue), the management abandoned the idea of a plot and reduced the framing story to reporters who are looking for stories in the city. The production was less successful than the previous ones, though it did not flop. Fejér saw this as an endorsement of his earlier approach, namely that 'there is no theatre without drama'.[175] With the blessing of the Ministry, Fejér ended his revue experiments after one season, and under his management, the Municipal Gaiety Theatre became the second theatre of operetta in Budapest. The Municipal Council summarised the season of experiments: 'This year, the theatre was looking for a way to create the "socialist revue", but the results were not satisfying. It proved that the rotted genre of the revue cannot be filled with socialist content'.[176]

---

[173] Shorthand report of the Stanislavski-circle meeting in the Municipal Gaiety Theatre, 8 February 1952, BFL VIII. 3806. 9. d.

[174] Comment of István Fejér at the professional preview of *Címe: ismeretlen*, 9 January 1952, OSZK SzT Fond 16/3.

[175] Comment of István Fejér at the season closing meeting of the Municipal Gaiety Theatre, 11 July 1952, OSZK SzT Fond 18/30.

[176] Minute book of the meeting of the Municipal Council 18 July 1952, BFL XXIII. 102. a. 1, 18.

5 Changes in Set and Costume Design: The Politics of Visual Representation

5.1 The Royal Building, Sets and Costumes

In 1949, the political leadership did not consider the Royal/Municipal Music Hall as representing the new cultural system. Hence, they did not invest in it, but neither did they demand its closure. When FŐNI took over its management, it attempted to modify both the exterior and the interior of the building to meet the (officially undeclared) political expectations. The stuccos of four naked women on the outside façade were removed or covered to signal a break with the traditional image of the house.[177] This façade was then specially decorated for holidays. On May Day, for example, giant portraits of Lenin, Stalin and Rákosi were installed. The headshots that once surrounded the entrance were replaced with pictures of ensemble scenes to replace 'star cult' with 'collectivism'. Nonetheless, the relative success of politicised pieces depended on casting well-known performers who kept their comedic styles intact. (Headshots of those who 'earned it' were installed in the foyer.) The auditorium itself also reflected the declared merits of the new society, as in a reserved box in the Grand Circle for the top workers of the Stakhanovite movement (*élmunkáspáholy*).

The Royal's stage measured 13 metres wide, 10.5 metres deep and 9 metres high.[178] Apart from the rigging loft, the theatre did not have any other stage apparatus, such as a revolving stage or trap doors. It did not even have a backstage or crossover area. These limitations drastically reduced the possibilities for visual effects. The only rehearsal space was the stage, which complicated daily operations.

Construction at the venue was constant due to the building's almost derelict condition. The management demanded a full engineering inspection because the floor sank in spots and the walls were cracking.[179] Karády pleaded with officials for a thorough renovation of the venue, but he barely got enough money for just the minor repairs. The fact that neither the Ministry nor the Council provided financial support indicates the political insignificance of the revue experiments.

The ways in which sets were designed and constructed did not change significantly after 1949, though designers and builders were burdened with an elaborate administration and, in theory, subordinated to political control. Sketches were

---

[177] Either the task was not completed, or new images of naked women were discovered because the order was repeated on 26 December. Minutes of the management meeting, 5 December 1949, BFL IV. 1521. FŐNI 1. d.

[178] Adressbuch (1943: 267).

[179] Letter from István Fejér and György Szilágyi to the Municipal Council, 15 November 1951, BFL XXIII. 114. 5. d.

supposed to be sent to the political superiors, but the visual aspects of a production were mostly examined by politicians attending previews.

Materials needed to build sets had to be ordered far ahead of when they were needed. Even so, there was no guarantee that any materials would be available due to general shortages. Whenever possible, materials had to be recycled. (Since FŐNI oversaw five venues, it was possible to rotate sets and recycle materials.) A set builder for the 1951 production of *7 vidám nap* (Seven Happy Days) vividly described the situation:

> The central [theatre workshop] had to complete sets for eight productions by the end of March, so they refused to do ours. If they had received the plans in February, they could have done it. So we started chasing down materials, which did not happen overnight ... We finally received the design for a backdrop which measured 54 square metres, so we had to move to the Népvarieté to paint it. We wanted to paint it on the floor but there was roof leakage and the materials got wet ... [I]t was so cold that the paint froze. ... We were finally allocated timber .. but we could not find any timber yard which had any in stock. On 24 March, we received 1,5 cubic meters of timber. ... On the 26th only small parts of the set were ready; opening on the 30th seemed hopeless. The management would not have opposed postponing the production because the libretto still wasn't ready. ... [But] the Council's order and love for theatre did not allow us to stop. ... We had to work day and night.[180]

Costuming practices remained as before nationalisation. The theatre provided costumes but performers had to bring their own street clothes as needed. With the shows becoming increasingly 'rooted in reality' and less abstract or glamorous, street clothes became the norm. Costume shops also had to deal with the lack of raw materials. Costumes and shoes belonging to the theatre could only be used in the final five rehearsals before the performances began in order to preserve them as much as possible. This did not help or please the performers, especially the dancers.

5.2 The Designer: Eric

The principal set and costume designer – and therefore the person responsible for the visual aspect of the revues – was known by the pseudonym Eric (born Imre Vogel, 1907–96). His career exemplifies how and to what extent talented and renowned artists had to adapt the work to meet political requirements and how this affected the creation of socialist revues. Rejected by the College of Applied Arts in Budapest, he studied at the Viennese *Kunstgewerbeschule*

---

[180] Minute book of the backstage worker's production meeting in the Municipal Music Hall, 17 April 1951, SZKL XII. 40. f. 225. ő. e.

between 1925 and 1927.[181] He took the pseudonym Eric by shortening the Germanised version of his given name, Emmerich. He returned to Budapest in 1927 and started working for operetta theatres. To make ends meet, he also worked as an illustrator for magazines and designed sheet music covers. Eric was offered a job at the Parisien Grill nightclub to redecorate it each week for its themed shows. In 1931, he began designing sets and costumes for the Moulin Rouge, something he continued to do until the late 1980s. Being Jewish, he was drafted for labour service twice during World War II; nonetheless, he kept designing for the Moulin Rouge. After 1945, he scrapped his plans for emigration when Teddy Ehrenthal asked him to design for the Royal as well as at the Moulin Rouge. From 1948, he also designed for the Operetta Theatre. After the communist takeover, Margit Gáspár decided not to employ him because she did not want to attach his style and his nightclub past to her operetta experiments. Karády then invited him to FŐNI. Eric's style is characterised by vivid palettes and idealised bodies: lean women with large breasts and athletic-looking men. He recalled one particular incident:

> I knew the bodies of actors and actresses and I knew what suited them. János Sárdy was the dream of women and when I had to make a Prince Bob out of him, I was shocked to see ... a seventeen-year-old boy: stick legs, narrow shoulders ... I added padding to his thighs, gave him 5 cm-high insoles, stuffed his shoulders – and the audience went wild.[182]

The sharp-tongued critic Péter Molnár Gál remarked: 'During the seventy years of his career he went out of fashion more times than others came into fashion'.[183] Eric and his work formed a continuity between the discarded professional tradition and the new principles.

5.3 Visual and Thematic Topoi in the FŐNI Revues

Neither the Municipal Council nor the Ministry of People's Education provided any substantive guidelines about the visual aspects of revues. The socialist-realist approach to design was detailed in a booklet for students at the College of Applied Arts. Sets, however, had to serve the reality created by the actors and 'have the same role as the background of a figurative composition'.[184] Aesthetic possibilities were reduced to a form of naturalism, where not much room was left for imagination. One designer, György Rajkai, remarked, 'Nowadays in our plays, we very often find a set of instructions in which the author specifies what

---

[181] See his biography in Molnár (2019a: 360–367).
[182] József Bőgel: Az élet illusztrátora. *Színház*, February 1997, p. 44–45.
[183] Molnár Gál (2001: 276). In the DDR, Wolf Leder (1906–2009) had a similar career. He designed for the Berlin Scala and Plaza before World War II; after the war and was the head designer of the state revue theatre Friedrichstadt-Palast from 1954 until 1992.
[184] Bercsényi (1954: 4).

sorts of trees he imagines for the set of a scene. So the sets should not depict nonsensical trees but, for instance, pines, locusts or oaks'.[185]

In the FŐNI revues, choreography took priority over design, unlike in the pre-war nightclub shows where the visual settings were more important. This new approach is evident in the Troika scene from *Májusfa* (Maypole) which overtly promoted Russian culture (see Figure 12).[186] Apart from not having materials to build a set, Eric had to keep the stage empty for the all-important dance. He therefore had to create the entire visual spectacle using a single backdrop and costumes. The Hungarian Dance Association noted: 'The costume designer [Eric] did not know the subject of the dance and used the beautiful designs of *Kurslin's Spring Dance* by the Pyatnitsky choir. He should have been told that the troika, which is a mode of winter transportation for the Russian people, has nothing to do with these costumes'.[187] Eric sacrificed authenticity in favour of spectacle. Also, it might have been easier to copy a Soviet design than to risk the criticism of the officials.

Several recurring thematic topoi appear in the *FŐNI* revues. These include Budapest itself, foreign countries and cultures, a taming of eroticism, new state-owned companies and Marxist representations of the past.

Figure 12 The Troika-scene from *Májusfa. Színház és Mozi*, 7 May 1950, p. 29.

---

[185] Rajkai (1954: 23). [186] A wider shot of the scene appears in Molnár (2020: 50).
[187] Ágnes Roboz's review of the Municipal Music Hall's new production (1950), OSZMI TA Bequest of Zsuzsa Ortutay 8. d. 2011. 10. 98.

The first of these, the reputation of Budapest as a global city, was politically appropriated for these revues. Budapest itself was tied to the idea of creating a socialist city that would represent the values of the new system. Popular locations such as the City Park or the Margaret Island were kept because of their nostalgic value, though their meanings were recontextualised. Since foreign tourism was basically non-existent, Budapest was now being advertised to the people of Budapest and visitors from the countryside. A didactic opposition of the city and village infuses many scenes, such as when a group of villagers comes to Budapest in *Jó reggelt, Budapest!* (Good Morning, Budapest!):

Zsiga: Did you see the Stalin Bridge? ...

Juci: And the new houses on Béke Square? Where everything is full of windows and sparkle ...

Feri: I wish she could come with me to see the construction of the Underground in front of the Stadium ...

Erzsike: And Feri could come with me to the Pioneer's Department Store.[188]

Visitors are thus being encouraged to visit new socialist landmarks in the city. The happy ending of *Jó reggelt, Budapest!* finds the lovers under the Stalin Bridge, which was dedicated two months before the show opened and where the lovers are certainly not alone.

Feri: (kisses Erzsi)

Policeman: (Steps out of the shadows, waits for the two to finish kissing) Well, I also wish you the best then! Congratulations!

Erzsi: (confused) Thank you, comrade!

Policeman: I patrol here each night ... and you are the 25th couple this evening to be here under the Stalin Bridge! I decided after the 10th that I would personally congratulate each happy couple. (Shakes hands with Feri and Erzsi) All the best! Be happy and take care of our beautiful city! Good night, comrades! (walks away)[189]

The revues' approach to foreign countries and cultures followed political dictates: East good – West bad. Countries and cultures of the Eastern Bloc could only be represented positively, ignoring any ethnic and economic conflicts. (Many Hungarians were still resenting their neighbours because of the borders set in Trianon and Paris.) Foreign cultures were represented mainly through dance scenes, which depended on the knowledge and often the imagination of Hungarian choreographers. The idea of travel only appeared in one revue, *Békehajó* (Ship of Peace).

---

[188] *Jó reggelt, Budapest!* – script. BFL VIII. 3806. 10. d.
[189] *Jó reggelt, Budapest!* – script. BFL VIII. 3806. 10. d.

The ship was not an ocean liner, which would have carried associations with cosmopolitanism, capitalism and the high life, but rather a warship. According to the story, Americans had captured a Hungarian ship in Marseilles and the Hungarian crew managed to regain control and sail home. This was despite the fact that Hungary had neither a military fleet nor access to the sea.[190] But beyond the Americans being the villains of the piece, the political side of the story was further strengthened when a 'protective Soviet cruiser' from the Black Sea accompanies the Hungarian ship on its journey home. The two ships visit several countries on their journey, but notably not Yugoslavia. Sailing on the Danube, the ship goes directly from Romania to Hungary, though Yugoslavia lies between. Because of the split between Yugoslavia's Tito and the USSR's Stalin, any references to Yugoslavia were omitted, and the country's existence was ignored.

Eroticism was a defining and popular feature of Hungarian revues before 1949. Discarding this was one of the few direct political mandates.[191] In the socialist revues, such elements were not completely removed but certainly made less overt. For example, in *Botrány az Állatkertben* (Scandal in the Zoo), the 'Tejcsárda (Milk Bar) Scene' ended with the dance of the six 'Baby girls'. Their swaddling clothes might not have generated immediate erotic associations but their fingers in their mouths certainly could. Such costumes were used in a more revealing version earlier in the Moulin Rouge (see Figures 13 and 14).

Concerning nudity, Karády remembered, 'There wasn't any. These so-called socialist morals ... it was out of the question to be topless or to wear anything transparent'.[192] This principle is evident in the 'Moroccan Fair Scene' from *Békehajó* (see Figure 15), which was the last explicit scene to appear in a socialist revue. Eric's trick was to use rhinestone and sequin decorations to emphasise the covered female figures. When it came to displays of love, these were limited to kisses on the lips, as in *Jó reggelt, Budapest!*[193]

Advertising the new, state-owned companies was a new political element in the revues. The aforementioned 'Milk Bar Scene' featured a set that included shelves of milk bottles and other dairy products standing in order, all crowned with the logo of the new state dairy company. While suggesting abundance, stores lacked even basic goods. If a state company was not represented with abundance, concerns were raised, as in this review of *Májusfa*: 'The set of the second scene in front of the Sporting Goods State

---

[190] Elements of the story (e.g., a ship in a foreign harbor in the hands of imperialists) resemble Dunayevsky's 1947 operetta Вольный ветер (Free Wind).
[191] Minute book of the Municipal Cultural Committee's session, 5 January 1950, BFL XXXV. 95. c. 4. 24. ő. e.
[192] Conversation with Béla Karády, 26 September 2013.
[193] *Jó reggelt, Budapest!* – script. BFL VIII. 3806. 10. d.

Figure 13 Eric's costumes for 'Baby girls' advertising the new state dairy company, Tejért, 1949.

Department is a mistake. ... Storefronts are absolutely unlike other storefronts. There isn't a single storefront in reality, where there are two shirts with a tennis court. In our regard, a storefront stuffed plentifully with goods should be painted and not a landscape'.[194] The 'Állami Áruház (State Department Store) Scene' in *Botrány az Állatkertben* celebrated the opening of the fiftieth state department store (see Figure 10). The main entrance and its storefront were painted on the backdrop in the style of a propaganda posters. The costumes were meant to depict the uniforms of the salesgirls; however, the length of the skirts was not that of their actual uniforms but rather what was typical of showgirls in a revue. This scene was a live advertisement that included the salesgirls throwing product samples to the audience. We do not have documentation as to whether the Ministry of Internal Commerce or the stores themselves proposed some form of collaboration with FŐNI; this might have been Karády's decision.

Finally, the past was reinterpreted according to vulgar Marxist views.[195] Although certain periods, such as the 1930s, could only appear in negative contexts, they were included because the audiences enjoyed them. Performing

---

[194] József Szőnyi's review of *Májusfa*, 20 April 1950, BFL XXIII. 114. 4. d.
[195] Several heavily politicised operettas, plays and films set in different periods were written at the time, for example, *Csínom Palkó*, an operetta by Ferenc Farkas. See Bozó (2020).

Figure 14 Eric's costumes for the showgirls of the Moulin Rouge in 1937.

such mockeries was often difficult and resulted in official complaints.[196] Self-reflection and parodying other shows used to be an essential part of pre-1949 productions but they were missing completely from socialist revues. So was

---

[196] 'Entertainment venues, after multiple written and verbal warnings, stubbornly stick to the rotten genre of the bourgeois revue.... Parodies and caricatures are mostly performed in a way that do not discredit but popularise [their subjects]'. Minute book of the Municipal Council's meeting, 6 June 1952, BFL XXIII. 102. a. 1. p 11.

Figure 15 'The Moroccan Fair' scene from *Békehajó*.

night-time and nightlife: Avoiding such references was the best way to distance the new productions from their condemned predecessors. The same thing happened with references to the *demimonde* (prostitution, criminality, etc.), which did not officially exist in the socialist utopia.

5.4 The Approach of the Municipal Gaiety Theatre

György Rácz, director of the Municipal Gaiety Theatre, thought that the visual dimension of socialist revues should offer a realistic spectacle:

> The set of the revue must closely comply with the author's intention, the style of the dance scenes and the mood of the music. . . . The designer does not have to recreate Margaret Island in its current state; he may mix elements to reflect Margaret Island in ten years' time and its future splendour. But he should never present leaves covered in gold glitter, velvet tree trunks and sequined arbours. . . . Without a doubt, such staples of our practice, like the stairs, the velvet, the coloured lights or even a flash of a nice pair of legs, should not be discarded, but revue realities cannot neglect the reality of life and its artistic requirements, which make no exceptions to rules that are strict and fixed, just like in every other genre.[197]

---

[197] Minute book of the conference *Kell-e revü és ha igen, milyen legyen?*, 17 February 1952, OSZK SzT Fond 16/4.

Rácz seems to have had a definite opinion of what to depict and how to depict it, though he remained flexible in his overall approach. He abandoned the visual aesthetic of earlier revues in favour of naturalism but still argued for the creative fantasy of the designer. Imagination was essential, especially when the designer was supposed to create a scene invented by writers. This was the case for the scene in *Most jelent meg* (The Latest Issue) in which the journalists visit a factory. The scenario espouses state propaganda on developing heavy industries:

> Scene 19. An iron foundry. A huge bowl flies in slowly from the left with dignity and lands in front of the furnace on the right. The old Miska, Kőrösi, Éva and the reporter are standing on the right side of the furnace. On the left a Worker holds a tapping rod in his hand. When a couple of seconds later Miska and Kőrösi set the bowl under the mouth of the tap, he [the Worker] smashes the clay lining inside the furnace and a river of molten white iron river bursts through the tap. Kőrösi stands proudly and watches their reflections in the river of fire emanating from the furnace.[198]

Unfortunately, we do not have any surviving images of this scene. The designer's task was to enliven narrative elements like 'watching their reflections in the river of fire' into a stage spectacle. This particular scene also required the designer to familiarise himself with the processes of ironworks in order to depict them accurately.

Although Eric ensured that several traditional topoi survived, his work was restricted by the text and the choreography. Revues lost their visual spectacle because of the required 'naturalism', and these new plot- and text-based productions were not that different from operettas. The socialist revue experiments ended in 1952 with the admission that it was impossible to find a type of revue that was acceptable to both the political leadership and the public. A new chapter in Hungarian political history, however, was about to begin, and with it came new chances for the revue.

6 The Recuperation and Stabilisation of Revues in Socialist Hungary after 1953

On 5 March 1953, Joseph Stalin died. The next year was marked by a major political change: Soviet leaders ordered Rákosi to step down and replaced him with the less radical Imre Nagy and a new government. Nagy introduced moderate reforms that improved overall living standards. Internment camps were closed and most of the political prisoners were released. However, Rákosi

---

[198] *Most jelent meg* – script. BFL VIII. 3806. 10. d.

(still the General Secretary of the Party) issued a counterattack and regained power a year later. His second tenure did not last long, for within a couple of months, Nikolai Khrushchev denounced the policies of Stalin and his personality cult.

On 23 October 1956, after police opened fire on a peaceful student demonstration, events escalated into a revolution against the Soviet regime. Two weeks later the Soviets invaded Hungary and put János Kádár (1912–89) in power. His name became synonymous with the era, for he remained General Secretary of the Hungarian Socialist Workers' Party (MSzMP) for the next thirty-two years. He began by demanding retribution from the insurgents and executing Imre Nagy. Kádár's policy changed in the early 1960s with the introduction of a milder form of authoritarianism that focused on raising living standards and depoliticising everyday life.

The government's attitude towards culture also changed, since the centralised system was clearly not sustainable.[199] The *új gazdasági mechanizmus* (New Economic Mechanism) was a major economic reform that the Party's Central Committee approved in 1966 and implemented in 1968. Individual enterprises achieved greater autonomy at the expense of central planners. Companies could decide what and how much they would produce and offer for sale; ultimately, profitability became the sole measure of a firm's success.[200] The system of censorship was also reformed. After 1956, the Hungarian government no longer ran censorship offices. Instead, responsibility for self-censorship was placed on editors, publishers and managers in the fields of culture and science.[201] The trusted party members put in charge knew which topics should be avoided.

During the 1960s, Hungary opened its borders to a wider circle of visitors. János Pap, Minister of the Interior between 1961 and 1963, recalled: 'We started opening the gates with the belief that tourism cannot be disadvantageous for a socialist country. We had to seriously change the picture of the enemy in the sense that not everyone is an enemy who wants to come here; not everyone is interested in our secrets'.[202] The number of tourists to Hungary increased dramatically from 37,121 in 1951 to 102,619 in 1955, 524,612 in 1960 and 6,319,617 in 1970.[203] This so-called *gulyáskommunizmus* (goulash communism), with its relative cultural freedom, earned Hungary the reputation of being the so-called 'happiest barracks of the Eastern Bloc'.

---

[199] Kalmár (2014: 254). [200] Balassa (1970: 4). See also Romsics (1999: 346).
[201] Kalmár (2014: 297). [202] Molnár (2014: 45).
[203] *Statistical Pocket Book of Hungary*, 1960: 119; 1974: 227.

6.1 International Tours

It took six years after the borders were sealed in 1949 before a Hungarian theatre could offer a foreign guest performance. The Operetta Theatre travelled to Moscow in 1955, where their major success was not one of their propaganda operettas but rather a rewritten version of *The Csárdás Princess*.²⁰⁴ A year later the first major 'exchange of artists' (*artistacsere*) was organised between Hungary and the Soviet Union. As part of this, a Hungarian *esztrád-együttes* (road company) was invited to Moscow. The Soviets and director Béla Karády selected the best politically eligible entertainers to join the troupe.²⁰⁵ The Ministry of People's Education organised celebrations in Budapest for both its departure and return, indicating the significance of the endeavour. The show's title, *Вечером в Будапеште* (An evening in Budapest) was not aggressively propagandistic but rather recalled the city's nightlife tradition (see Figure 16). The political situation even two years earlier would not have allowed such a title. The production's reception at the Teatr Estrady in Moscow was more than enthusiastic: Karády proudly reported that the company received 'thirteen

Figure 16 Poster for *Вечером в Будапеште* (Tour of the Hungarian Estrada Company) at the Teatr Estrady, Moscow, 1956.

---

²⁰⁴ This was followed by two further invitations in 1962 and 1968. On the reworked production of *The Csárdás Princess*, see Heltai (2011a: 295–324).

²⁰⁵ Bogár, n. d.: 63.

thunderous ovations'[206] per show. The ten-week run sold out in one day. Forty shows were planned but the final number of performances was sixty-one, and the production was seen by about 400,000 people. The cast even appeared on television; such was its popularity.

The performers used the rare opportunity of travelling to buy appliances unavailable in Hungary at the time, including televisions, refrigerators and washing machines.[207] More importantly, visiting the Soviet Union provided first-hand experience as to how show business worked in what was deemed the model for Hungary. As an official report stated, '[W]e still have a lot to learn regarding how we can be more courageous with our own possibilities of entertainment'.[208]

The tour was a definite hit. Karády remembered,

> 'It was such a success that we immediately signed a contract for the following year. But in the meantime the Revolution happened, so I thought of this as *passé*. And in the spring of '57 ... when there was still hardly any theatre life, I received a call from the [Soviet] Embassy asking when we were leaving and what's in the show. ... It was difficult to put [the show] together because some said that they were not willing [to participate]'.[209]

The second tour in March 1957 was longer than the first one, lasting two months and playing 144 performances in twenty-six different cities. Titled *Будапештские Открытки* (Budapest Postcards), it was organised under the auspices of the Országos Cirkusz Vállalat (National Circus Company), which noted: '[T]he former leadership of the Institute for Cultural Relations declared that our only job was to sign the contract, the rest was theirs. This is how Béla Karády became director of the company. ... [H]e put the show together in a way that it only reflected American jazz'.[210] This jazz focus met with slight criticism in the Soviet press.[211] Still, tours to the Soviet Union continued in the following years (June 1959, July 1960 and December 1963), although each became progressively less a show and more a pop concert.

Few sources document entertainment in Budapest during the two weeks of the 1956 Revolution (23 October–4 November). The Budapest Kávéház (Moulin Rouge) closed at 2 p.m. daily because of a curfew. The dancer Richárd Bogár

---

[206] *Vastaps* in the original. This is a type of strong rhythmic applause where the entire audience claps in unison. Originally, this indicated the public's demand to see the actors or the author of the piece again after their bows. In the 1950s, it became a forced behaviour to celebrate political speeches. Nowadays, it has lost its original meaning and is the default applause style of Hungarian audiences.

[207] Bogár, n. d.: 67.   [208] Jazz és revü a Szovjetunióban, *Új Világ*, 23 August 1956, p. 6.

[209] Conversation with Béla Karády, 26 September 2013.

[210] Egy szovjet turné tanulságai, *Film Színház Muzsika*, 12 July 1957, p. 9.

[211] Н. Барзилович: Вечером в Будапеште, *Вечерняя Москва*, 15 March 1957, p. 3.

recalled those days: 'Everybody's planning and swearing that they will leave the country tomorrow. ... We say that we'll meet tomorrow at Kärtnerstraße [in Vienna]. We shake hands. We drink. The next day we definitely greet each other again in the Budapest Kávéház and laugh'.[212] Several entertainment professionals, though, did leave the country, including directors Tamás Fellegi and Vilmos Lóránth; actresses Violetta Ferrari, Juci Hódossy, Ida Boros, Magda Kardos, Erzsi Rév and Ida Turay; comedians István Békeffi and Imre Halmai; and magician Pál Potassy.

In the years after the revolution, several French performers appeared in Hungary, some of whom were major entertainers. In February 1957, the singer Lucienne Boyer performed in Budapest, and the next month Yves Montand gave a concert and generously donated his payment of 1.5 million Francs to the Hungarian Red Cross to aid victims of the Revolution.[213] An ice revue, *Paris sur glace*, visited twice, in 1957 and in 1962, and in June 1958, the legendary Josephine Baker returned for her fourth and final visit and concert in Budapest. The reason why this happened specifically with French performers is unclear. Perhaps it was connected to the powerful French Communist Party's (PCF) visit in June 1957 supporting the Soviet invasion of Hungary and the new government.

A different sort of French connection came through Michel Gyarmathy (born Miklós Ehrenfeld, 1908–96), who, after designing for Budapest operetta theatres, emigrated to Paris in 1936. He eventually became director of the internationally renowned Folies Bergère revues. His success was reported in the Hungarian press since 1958, despite the fact that the aesthetics of the *Folies* would be impossible to emulate in Budapest, especially having fully naked performers on stage. From the early 1960s, he and his Folies revues became regular stops for Hungarian tourists in Paris, not just his former professional colleagues but also ordinary people. Part of this was because he provided free tickets to his countrymen. His shows were the best that an average Hungarian could see at the time. As Karády remarked, 'One of Gyarmathy's castoff costumes is a star costume in Pest'.[214] Gyarmathy had been including Hungarian folk-themed scenes in his revues since 1946 not only because of his love for his homeland but also because such acts were immensely popular in foreign productions.[215]

---

[212] Bogár, n. d.: 71.

[213] 5 perc Yves Montand-al Budapesten, *Népakarat*, 14 February 1957, p. 1.

[214] Conversation with Béla Karády, 26 September 2013. Gyarmathy was not the only Hungarian involved with post-war Parisian revues (Jenő Pataki hosted and György Lugosi directed shows in La Nouvelle Eve), but Gyarmathy became a Hungarian 'celebrity' and his shows were reviewed.

[215] For an analysis of the 'Hungarian' theme, see Molnár (2019b: 221–224).

In the DDR (East Germany), Hungarian artists began to appear in 1953 as part of a series of inter-state artistic exchanges. From the 1960s, many Hungarian dancers gave guest performances and had life-long careers in the DDR.[216] The Friedrichstadt-Palast, the state-owned and controlled revue theatre in Berlin, was in a completely different cultural position than the theatres in Budapest. It was a leading light in legitimate East German cultural life. The first Hungarian collaboration with the Friedrichstadt-Palast took place in May 1960. *Budapester Melodie* (Budapest Melody) featured exclusively Hungarian artists as well as Béla Rácz and his Gypsy Orchestra, who had been active in Budapest nightlife during the 1930s. The Palast's next Hungarian show was *Budapester Nächte* (Budapest Nights) in 1964, the title of which directly alluded to the city's nightclub tradition, presumably to attract tourists (see Figure 17). The Friedrichstadt-Palast's guest performances in Hungary (in 1966 and 1969) received rave reviews in the Hungarian press. Critics lamented why Budapest did not have a revue theatre like the Friedrichstadt-Palast.[217]

6.2 A New Revue Experiment

In 1960, the tiny Budapest Varieté was closed. The dedicated Revűszínház (revue theatre) was considered to be established in the old swimming pool-turned-cinema-turned-theatre, the former home of the Fővárosi Víg Színház. Tarka Színpad (Colourful Stage) ultimately produced seven revues, all of which could be regarded as further failed attempts of the socialist state to make stage revues part of Hungarian cultural life. The legitimacy of the genre was not questioned anymore, only its form. The idea of 'educative entertainment' was still theoretically present, but it was no longer an explicit political requirement.[218]

The first production, *Játsszunk valami mást* (Let's play something else; 19 November 1960), was staged by György Rácz, who directed the last socialist revues. It received universally negative reviews, which kept several directors away from subsequent productions. Although Rácz insisted on maintaining a frame story – a writer and a director wandering in Budapest looking for material – textual elements no longer dominated the show. It was the individual acts that mattered, even though established professionals of the genre were not involved. In addition to unfulfilled expectations for stage spectacle, reviewers

---

[216] For example, György Klapka, Ferenc Salmayer and László Karikás. After the building of the Berlin Wall, dancers who stayed in the West had to be replaced. This allowed Emőke Pöstényi to become the esteemed choreographer at the Friedrichstadt-Palast and of the show dance ensemble of the East German Television (DFF). Pöstenyi, 2020: 27.
[217] Világszerte siker a revü – és Budapesten? *Hétfői Hírek*, 31 October 1966, p. 6. A nagyváros romantikája, *Esti Hírlap*, 31 January 1967, p. 2. Palastrevü '69, *Tükör*, 5 August 1969, p. 18.
[218] Vitányi (1965: 228).

Figure 17 Poster for *Budapester Nächte*, March 1964.

also complained that the curtain had to be lowered for several minutes during scene changes.[219] The venue itself was unsuitable because of its relatively small size and lack of stage machinery. After the second production, the management issued a statement:

> We did not want to establish a revue theatre, but rather a higher standard of music hall. Revues do not have a tradition in Hungary. ... We talk a lot about

---

[219] Tibor Bános: Játsszunk tényleg valami mást! *Hétfői Hírek*, 21 November 1960, p. 4.

the future; we are looking at possibilities for the genre. We would like to create a tasteful music hall show with many revue elements. This is what we can do and this aligns with our ideas.[220]

The management might have been aware of the revue tradition in Hungary (what this Element has already shown), however, neither traditional nor experimental revues could have been cited as reference points in 1960 due to the delicate political situation. Plans for building a new revue theatre were still being discussed, but it was expensive and not a priority for politicians.[221] Opening the Tarka Színpad was to be a partial solution to the problem, which ultimately did not satisfy the public and closed in 1963.

Parallel to what was happening at the Tarka Színpad, another experiment was underway at the Petőfi Színház (Petőfi Theatre), where they were targeting young audiences in order to create the Hungarian musical. Although these government-supported experiments were abandoned in 1964, musicals were considered progressive and modern, as opposed to operettas, which were not. The debate between the two approaches, some of which took place on television,[222] dominated the public discourse about musical theatre. In 1968, Béla Karády, at the time the artistic leader of the Magyar Cirkusz és Varieté Vállalat (Hungarian Circus and Music Hall Company), was still envisioning new directions for the revue:

> [W]e cannot discard the rich costume and set design fantasies of the Western revue, the music of global hits and the presence of truly fashionable dance styles; but each minute of the show has to reflect our ideology of building socialism and the daily matters of our people in accord with the Party's policy.[223]

It remains unknown how seriously Karády was reconsidering a politicised version of the genre. His later *Moulin Rouge* revues (*Horoszkóp '72*, 1972, *Csudapesti éjszaka*, 1973) did not contain any political references. It is likely, therefore, that Karády's political speech pattern was just part of the required rhetoric, just as it had been in the 1950s. His lobby for a new theatre was unsuccessful: controlling the emerging youth culture of the 1960s was more of a concern for politicians. The Hungarian Television announced the first

---

[220] Jegyzetek és kérdések az Űrmacska ürügyén. *Film Színház Muzsika*, 24 March 1961, p. 28.
[221] A nagyváros romantikája, *Esti Hírlap*, 31 January 1967, p. 2. Defying hopes, the reconstruction of the Municipal Grand Circus building (1966–1971) was also not planned to serve as a revue theatre.
[222] In 1967, the TV special *Pompadour bikiniben* (Pompadour in bikini) showcased the rivalry of the two genres, concluding that they are the same. The programme was the idea of operetta performer and advocate Róbert Rátonyi. See Rátonyi (1984: 389).
[223] Béla Karády: Beszélgessünk a revűről (ami nincs). KGY 68–69.

Táncdalfesztivál (Dance Song Contest) in 1966, as a part of the domestication process of the counterculture manifested in beat music.[224] The contests were watched by millions, compared to which the question of a new revue theatre seemed hardly relevant. Furthermore, television revues (e.g., *Csudapest*, 1962) offered such spectacles, which stage revues could not.

6.3 Socialist Striptease

Nightclub shows, on the other hand, were enjoying a revival in the 1960s. As border crossing became easier, in 1961, the Budapest City Council was discussing the possibility of increasing foreign tourism. The state recognised the financial benefits, but the poor condition of the hospitality and night-time entertainment industries (hotels, nightclubs, etc.) was a concern: 'The evening and nightlife downtown are desolate. The existing entertainment venues can no longer satisfy even the local demand. There isn't a single venue or nightclub of international standards that foreigners ... could visit'.[225] To promote tourism, the City Council needed to find 'a crafty and smart way to attract [tourists] and to provide an opportunity to squeeze out [their hard] currency'.[226] The term *világvárosi műsor* (global city show) was reinstated as a goal and later as a recurring tagline for major nightclubs. As in the 1920s, neon lights were installed to make the city more attractive[227] which was further promoted by a multilanguage photo book.[228] In 1964, a new bus tour called 'Budapest by Night' was introduced, which showcased consumer-focused nightlife 'from the corner pub to the Táncpalota (Moulin Rouge)'[229] (see Figures 18 and 19). Meanwhile, another phenomenon was challenging the stern cultural policy: striptease.

From the late 1950s, striptease shows and acts were increasingly being discussed in official reports, travelogues and film reviews, where they were depicted as deviant products of the West. Following the cultural approach of the Stalinist period, striptease was seen as a dubious genre that existed merely for sexual arousal without any 'meaning' or 'message'.[230] By that time, show

---

[224] Kappanyos (2017).
[225] The planning of the city centre, composite description. Minute book of the Municipal Council's meeting, December 1964, BFL XXIII.101.a.1, p. 123.
[226] Minute book of the Municipal Council's meeting, 21 September 1961, HU BFL XXIII.102.a.1, p. 222. The Moulin Rouge featured in the first Hungarian guidebook to appear since the 1940s, see Boldizsár (1956: 368).
[227] Moulin Rouge és Hófehérke, *Magyar Nemzet*, 26 August 1959. The article, which also thought that the Arizona Club would be reopened, was reprinted in the *New York Times*. 'Neon signs to light Budapest's streets', *New York Times*, 20 September 1959, p. 131.
[228] Czeizing (1961).
[229] Report on the touristic situation of the capital and its further tasks, 3 December 1964, BFL XXIII.101.a.1, p. 14.
[230] 'Helyeselhetjük-e a sztriptízt?' *Világ Ifjúsága*, 1 January 1965, p 7.

Figure 18 Façade of the Budapest Táncpalota (Budapest Dance Palace), the former Moulin Rouge, 1958. Fortepan / Sándor Bauer 111439.

Figure 19 Interior of the Budapest Kávéház before remodelling, 1957. Fortepan / Sándor Bauer

dancers' costumes had been extremely revealing which raised the question: If the shows were allowed to be so erotic, why was stripping not allowed? During the first half of the 1960s, striptease became a crystallised symbol of the difference between the West and the East. It emblemised the question of living standards: what do *they* have and what do *we* have? Striptease asked whether Hungary could keep up with the latest global styles and trends, especially since it already existed in other socialist countries.

Just as revues had to establish their legitimacy within socialist culture a decade earlier, striptease now faced a similar challenge. Its only validation was popular demand, but neither the Party nor cultural leaders provided guidance on how to approach it, leaving unanswered questions about the role of entertainment. Were the products of the entertainment business still required to be 'meaningful' – that is, 'educational', as was the case after 1949 – or could they simply be entertaining, as they were before 1949? By the 1960s, this 'meaning' no longer referred to aggressive ideological propaganda aimed at proving moral superiority over the West.

The fact, that there was no response from the cultural administration encouraged managers and directors to experiment with striptease. The small Kamara Varieté produced a striptease-themed show in the spring 1967 that did not include any actual stripping. It did not generate any political repercussions, and the press did not condemn it.[231] This suggested that maybe more could be done. István Barna (1920–93) began as a waiter in the Moulin Rouge, where he rose to be manager in a couple of years. By 1968, he was the head of communications and show producer of Pannónia, the state hospitality company, where he staged a stripping act. He took precautions: the act was not staged in a major establishment or in a venue considered to be 'dubious'. An invited press preview would test audience reactions and the show was called a 'parody' so that if there were negative reactions, he could claim that it was all meant to be a satire or a joke. As for the 'meaning' of the production, the aspect which made the show different from a Western one, the act included a stylised setting and a narrative. *Sztriptíz paródia* (Striptease parody) opened at one of the newly built catering and entertainment venues, the Európa Restaurant, in July 1967.[232] One reviewer described the act:

> A young lady entered the properly obscured stage wearing an evening gown and sat on a sofa prepared for her. Due to the darkness, she might have thought it was already nighttime, so she started her bedtime routine.

---

[231] 'Sztrip10 a Kamara Varietében' *Népszava*, 7 April 1967, p. 2.
[232] Lajos H. Barta: Gyom. *Magyar Nemzet*, 19 July 1967, p. 3.

> At the same time, she was reading a detective novel in which a burglar entered to complete her undressing; but at the last moment there was a blackout ... and [when the lights came back on] the artist was already wearing a robe.[233]

Because of the lack of repercussions, this narrative-based, no-nudity stripping ('striptease Hungarian style' as the reviewer journalist put it) soon appeared in several nightclub shows. Nevertheless, it was ridiculed in the press[234] and within six months this added 'meaning' was abandoned in favour of the classic style.

The journalist-comedian Ferenc Ősz tried to obtain a statement from either the City Council or the Ministry of Culture regarding striptease, but without success. The responses he did receive from a district officer reflected the uncertainty of the situation:

Ferenc Ősz (FŐ): What do you think of strip-tease?

District Officer (DO): There's a demand for it, so I do not question its right to exist.

FŐ: Do you mean that whatever is in demand can be done?

DO: No ... no ... not exactly ... well, anyway, what we have is not real stripping.

FŐ: And you are to give the go-ahead to real stripping in the next programme they submit to you?

DO: I shall consult my superiors.

FŐ: Can't you decide on your own?

DO: I told you there are no regulations on this matter. I must be able to support my refusal by reference to something.

FŐ: Why not to your own official authority, or your own taste?

DO: That's a very naive way of looking at it. The district next door might well have given permission already. What we need in this matter is some kind of coordination of opinion to guide us.[235]

As the exchange reveals, each district council had the authority to decide whether or not to permit striptease. Since the situation was unclear, wrong decisions could mean councillors losing their jobs. This uncertainty challenged also those, who believed in the system. The aforementioned District Officer added: 'I've been in popular culture for twenty years now. Just think how many times I've had to readjust to a new line. I know as well as any one

---

[233] Tamás Garai: Sztriptíz magyar módra. *Ország-Világ*, 27 December 1967, p. 22.
[234] Tamás Földes: Indokolt vetkőzés. *Élet és Irodalom*, 25 May 1968, p. 6.
[235] Ferenc Ősz: Sztriptíz magyar módra. *Élet és Irodalom*, 18 May 1968, p. 12. The cited English edition: Strip-tease Hungarian style. *New Hungarian Quarterly* 10, no. 33 (spring 1969), p. 221.

Figure 20 Eva Sorg's striptease at the Savoy Bar, 1967. Fortepan / Sándor Bojár 180356.

(sic) that changes have had to be made in a great many things, but as things are I can't really be sure nowadays whether I'm taking a step forward or back'.[236]

At least part of the reason why striptease was being allowed could have been the fact that a major, legitimate state company, Pannónia, was producing shows. The fact that they did not generate any political backlash made them spread quickly. In May 1968, only four clubs had strip shows,[237] but by 1969, only four of Budapest's twenty-one clubs did not[238] (see Figure 20). Striptease's meteoric rise was being covered in English-language papers. In Britain, a report on Hungary named Budapest 'the Communist world's capital in, of all things, striptease'.[239] David Binder wrote in the *New York Times* that a real 'sex wave' was the consequence of allowing striptease in Hungary (looking at the rapid spread of explicitly sexual shows, this could be an accurate assessment). The reporter's source, an unnamed Hungarian journalist said, 'They argued that the

---

[236] Ferenc Ősz: Sztriptíz magyar módra. *Élet és Irodalom*, 18 May 1968, p. 12. Tibor Bános is a perfect example of this, who publicly condemned striptease in 1957, but praised *Kamara Varieté* for its *Sztrip10* and *Hungarosex* productions ten years later as 'keeping up with the change of times'. See Tibor Bános: Streap-tease (sic) a pesti utcákon! *Magyarország*, 11 September 1957, p. 10. cf. Tibor Bános: Utolsó mohikán. *Magyarország*, 31 December 1967, p. 27.
[237] Ferenc Ősz: Sztriptíz magyar módra. *Élet és Irodalom*, 18 May 1968, p. 12.
[238] István Pintér: Egy idegen az éjszakában, *Népszabadság*, 12 October 1969, p. 9.
[239] Strip-tease is approved in Hungary, *Coventry Evening Telegraph*, 23 September 1969, p. 11.

Vatican had approved striptease and therefore, People's Hungary should tolerate it too'.[240]

Aside from striptease, the Hungarian nightclub industry as a whole was being reinvigorated in the late 1960s and early 1970s. Between 1966 and 1968, new hotels and venues were being opened or renovated, such as the Béke Kupola, the Pezsgő Bár and the Éden Bár in Siófok. The only newly built venue in Budapest was the Maxim Varieté, which opened in 1972. It was the result of a personal lobby by István Barna, who became its manager and his wife the *meneuse* (house star).[241]

The Budapest Táncpalota reclaimed its old name, the Moulin Rouge. It opened at 10 p.m. and shows began at midnight. The house employed an eight-member orchestra, but for many performers it was the secondary (or tertiary) workplace, having contracts at other theatres. Shows were planned for long runs of 150 to 200 performances, and in the 1970s, only one spectacle was produced each year.[242] The theatre's international reputation could not be compared to what it was in the 1930s, and the 'new' Moulin Rouge held hardly any cultural significance among the Hungarian public. Although shows still targeted local middle-aged audiences,[243] the primary focus was on the tourist trade. The generation of creatives who made the house internationally famous in earlier times had by now retired.[244]

The zenith of the revues' cultural relevance has passed: new forms of entertainment appeared or became accessible which restructured taste and cultural consumerism. When revues became a 'legitimate' part of cultural life, they lost most of their relevance. The country's financial situation and political priorities made it possible to revive what was lost in 1952.

7 Epilogue: The Legacy of the Stalinist-Era Revue in Hungary

The core question behind introducing a novel type of entertainment in Hungary was not its content but rather its origin. If the narrative surrounding Hungarian revues in 1925 was not that they were new and foreign but rather something 'organically Hungarian', their reception might have been different. The issue was the same in the state-socialist context: the main problem was not what happened on stage but the fact that the entertainment sector and its genres were ignored when the new cultural structure was created. Should the Party's

---

[240] David Binder, 'Proletarian sex', *New York Times*, 29 June 1968, p. 2.
[241] See its layout and technical equipment in Szabó-Jilek (2022).
[242] See a comparison with Prague and East Berlin in Hansjürgen Pfeiler: 'Sie waren nicht in Budapest'. *Artistik*, January 1968, p. 11.
[243] István Pintér: Egy idegen az éjszakában. *Népszabadság*, 12 October 1969, p. 9.
[244] About the generational change see Bogár, n. d.: 88.

politicians have had a different image of entertainment venues and revues, these could have become integral parts of cultural life, as happened in other socialist countries. The same question surrounded striptease, but with a different result. Unlike revues, stripping was introduced by a producer for a major state company, which led to its acceptance. Yet this could not have happened without the cultural-economic reforms that sought to revive and financially exploit international tourism and provide a higher standard of living in Hungary.

7.1 Mentality

The state system provided secure employment for politically selected performers and no one else. Those allowed to work remained defenceless against theatre managers, especially since they were unable to move to another venue or employer. Performers had to tolerate managers. As the dancer Richárd Bogár recalled:

> It happened during the season [1947/48?] that the creators of the show were planning some sort of animal dance for a musical sequence. I don't remember what kind of animal costume and mask I should have worn, but I felt such disgust that I said I was not willing to do that. ... Teddy Ehrenthal wanted to fire me immediately. ... I was not fired but Teddy Ehrenthal ignored me and looked through me thereafter.[245]

An affair like this in the state theatre system likely had a defining effect on one's career. Theatre managers in turn depended on their political superiors. Such positions were reserved for politically trusted cadres. Being selected and put in charge of a theatre suggested that as long as one was loyal to the system, they would remain untouchable. This practice, of course, often led to a misuse of power.[246] The expression '*felmegyek a miniszterhez*' (I will see the Minister) was more than just the title of a 1962 film: it was common practice. When Bogár was choreographing a show in 1963, one of the dancers received a draft notice.

> I decided to go to the Ministry myself to talk with the officer responsible for military affairs. [Theatre manager] Emil Petrovics and financial manager Róna agreed to come with me. The next morning, we contacted the military affairs officer of the Ministry of Cultural Affairs. We had a short talk but did not get a straight answer; even so, our impression was that nothing happened concerning the case and nothing would happen. ... Desperate, I decided to make a bold move: I would go to the first undersecretary – it was commonly known that he was one of the main managers of cultural affairs. ... We checked in with his assistant, telling her we were there to discuss an

---

[245] Bogár, n. d.: 24.
[246] The actress Ida Boros was harrassed by two different theatre managers within two years. Molnár (2019a: 183–193).

extremely important case. We were seated ... and the assistant announced that we'd been given two minutes.... [The undersecretary] shook hands with Róna and Petrovics, exchanged a couple of words with them about their families and health and gave me a probing look when I introduced myself.... I explained what a great production we were preparing and that it would collapse if one of my dancers was drafted. He listened and wasn't affected at all.... [H]e reminded us about the military duty of citizens ... and asked me: 'Tell me, do you know Solymosi, the wing-back of the national football team?' ... 'Yes, I do.' ... 'You see? He was drafted too!' ... 'I'm sorry, but you misunderstood me.' He became suspicious. 'I did not ask for an exemption; just let him out for the training and the match like you do Solymosi.' He was surprised, smiled for a moment, changed the subject again to personal matters of Róna and Petrovics ... and said goodbye. ... I looked at Petrovics and Róna in the corridor. 'What now?' 'What what? It's done.' they told me.[247]

It was not only the entertainment business but also the entire theatre industry that relied on interpersonal and family connections. György Rácz, who directed the third wave of experimental revues, remembered: 'My mother was working in the financial department of the National Theatre, and I was the omnipotent (!) artistic leader of the Municipal Gaiety Theatre. One day my mother asked me if we could take a look at the young son of the secretary of Tamás Major [manager of the National Theatre], who wanted to be a dancer at all costs'.[248] Although the young man did not pass the audition, he would not have even had the opportunity without the family networks.

Karády described how decisions were made at the time: 'The Erzsébet pub was in front of the Royal ... [and] every evening after the show we met to have dinner and a beer; the things that mattered were decided there, not in management meetings. Over espresso, at dinner or while having a beer'.[249] In the 1970s, the top managers of the MACIVA [the state circus company] would join Karády for one day of his holidays at Balatonszéplak to plan the budget for the next year. As Karády noted, 'It could not have been done any other way'.[250]

These accounts imply a different, 'hidden' layer of Hungarian theatre history, one known only within professional circles and not among the public. The theatre system has continued to change, but public (mostly state) sponsorship and ownership remain defining features of the Hungarian theatrical sphere, especially when it comes to musical theatres. This layer, inherited from the socialist transformation of the sphere, still exists and is essential to understand the mechanisms and dynamics of contemporary Hungarian theatre.

---

[247] Bogár, n. d.: 126–128.   [248] Rácz (1984: 191).
[249] Conversation with Béla Karády, 30 January 2014.
[250] Conversation with Béla Karády, 30 January 2014.

7.2 A Forgotten Breaking Point

When looking at the number of performances for experimental socialist revues, several ran longer than many shows from the private era. *Békehajó* (Ship of Peace), for example, played more than 100 times during its run at the Municipal Music Hall in 1950; the last time a show played that long at that theatre was in 1933. In 1951, *Címe: ismeretlen* (Recipient: Unknown) ran even longer at 141 performances. These long runs – normally considered successes in a commercial sense – must be considered in terms of the small number of entertainment venues, the fact that factories brought their workers to performances and the relative financial security provided by municipal and state subsidies. Furthermore, many top performers were simply not allowed to appear anywhere else, and private theatres would not have been able to afford them, even if such opportunities would have been available. Compared to the performers, the creatives were in a better position. Although they were often replaced and moved from venue to venue, these were largely rhetorical moves, for their number was too small for a thorough political filtering. Thus, despite all efforts to eliminate them, several elements of the Budapest boulevard tradition were preserved in the socialist era.

For theatre professionals it was clear from the beginning that political requirements could not be fulfilled while maintaining audience numbers. Fearing negative consequences, established professionals tried to make the most out of the situation. Newcomers were placed in charge, most of whom remained in show business until their deaths. Sixty years later, Karády recalled, 'Those of us who made theatre were professionals. For us, neither ideology nor politics was the main thing, that was just the necessary evil in the background. The main thing was that the audience would buy tickets and from this, professional creators could make a living, preferably a good one'.[251]

Karády's mentor (and manager of the Operetta Theatre), the loyal communist Margit Gáspár, would have likely disagreed. Karády was driven to have a career. This highlights perhaps the main obstacle to the political acceptance of the revue: the lack of a prominent communist intellectual willing to 'legitimise' the genre. The revue's flexibility and ambiguous nature in the public consciousness were also disadvantages in the heavily regulated state-controlled theatre system.

The socialist revue experiments from the 1950s through the 1960s have largely disappeared from the collective cultural memory. The song from *Békehajó*, 'Budapest, te csodás' (Budapest, you are wonderful) by operetta composer Szabolcs Fényes is perhaps the only title that is still known, and it is divorced from its origin. (The song has been a Hungarian turbo-folk standard

---

[251] Conversation with Béla Karády, 30 January 2014.

since the late 1980s.) A smaller tabloid, *Ádám Magazin*, published a couple of pictures of FŐNI revues in 1979, but it was the 1930s revue culture that enjoyed a revival in the 1980s. The inspiration was probably Bob Fosse's film version of *Cabaret*, which premiered in Hungary in 1974. The first Budapest stage production of the musical followed in 1977, with several others appearing across the country. In 1981, the stage show *Miss Arizona* was produced about the tragic end of the *Arizona* club. *Kaméleon* (Chameleon), a musical based on the history of Hungarian musical theatre and the experiences of Richárd Bogár, played at the Municipal Operetta Theatre in 1984. The 1988 film version of *Miss Arizona* was an attempt to create a Hungarianised *Cabaret*, but despite Hanna Schygulla in the title role and Marcello Mastroianni as her husband, these well-known stars could not make the film a success, even in Hungary. The Moulin Rouge closed in 1989, and the Maxim followed in 1994. The rise of so-called 'ruin pubs' in the mid-2000s resembled the vivid club culture of the 1930s in many regards, though without the live shows. Recent stage productions called 'revue' in Hungary are little more than anachronistic imitations of a poorly imagined display of interwar aesthetics.[252] Revues are no longer associated with musical spectacle but with showgirls and feathers, while grand spectacles with celebrity casts such as *A játékkészítő* (The Toy Maker, 2014) emulate classic Hungarian revues more than their feathered and glittered distant cousins.

---

[252] For example, the November 2014 performance of the Municipal Grand Circus and the *Ooh la la* 'Night Revue Circus' at the Margaret Island Open Air Stage in July 2015.

References

Archives

Állambiztonsági Szolgálatok Történeti Levéltára (Historical Archives of State Security Services, ÁBTL)
Budapest Főváros Levéltára (Budapest City Archives, BFL)
Magyar Nemzeti Levéltár Országos Levéltára (Hungarian National Archives, MNL OL)
Országos Széchényi Könyvtár, Színháztörténeti Tár (National Széchényi Library, Theatre History Collection, OSZK SzT)
Országos Színháztörténeti Múzeum és Intézet, Táncarchívum (National Theatre History Museum and Institute, Dance Archives, OSZMI TA)
Politikatörténeti és Szakszervezeti Levéltár (Archive of Political History and Trade Unions, PIL SZKL)
Béla Karády Bequest (KGY Folder Name)

Oral Histories

Conversations with Béla Karády, 26 September 2013, 30 January 2014, 27 October 2014, 16 September 2015.
Conversation with Egon Lázár, 7 June 2015.

Parliamentary Documents

Képviselőházi Napló 1927
Nemzetgyűlési Napló 1920, 1922
Magyarországi Rendeletek Tára 1925, 1927

Newspapers and Periodicals

8 Órai Ujság 1925
Artisták Lapja (Magyar Artisták Lapja – Revue Artistique) 1920, 1921, 1939, 1942, 1946
Artistik 1968
Az Ujság naptára 1919
Az Est 1925, 1935
Budapesti Hírlap 1929
Coventry Evening Telegraph 1969

Élet és Irodalom 1968
Élet és Tudomány 1956
Esti Hírlap 1967
Esti Kurír 1925, 1926, 1929, 1931
Esti Ujság 1944
Fejér Megyei Hírlap 1968
Film Színház Muzsika 1957, 1961
Függetlenség 1944
Fővárosi Közlöny 1944, 1946
Hétfői Hírek 1960, 1966
Magyarország 1934, 1937, 1957, 1967
Magyarság 1944
Magyar Nemzet 1959, 1967
Magyar szó 1966
Melody Maker, The 1937
Nemzeti Ujság 1944
Neues Wiener Tagblatt 1927
New Hungarian Quarterly 1969
New York Times 1959, 1968
Népakarat 1957
Népszabadság 1969
Népszava 1942, 1967
Observer, The, 1927
Ország-Világ 1967
Paris-Midi 1927
Pesti Hírlap 1942
Pesti Napló 1924, 1928
Színház 1997
Színházi Élet 1919, 1920, 1936
Színház és Mozi 1949
Tükör 1969
Ujság 1927, 1928, 1937, 1941
Új Világ 1956
Variety 1934
Вечерняя Москва 1957
Világ 1920, 1922
Világ Ifjúsága 1965
Vogue 1939

Discography

Dezső Gyárfás: *Látta-e már Budapestet éjjel?* Dacapo-Record – O-5160, ca. 1908.

Joséphine Baker: *Dis-moi Joséphine*. Columbia – ESRF 1081, 1956.

Filmography

As you desire me, directed by George Fitzmaurice. Metro-Goldwyn-Mayer, 1932.

Csudapest, directed by István Deák. Magyar Televízió, 1962.

Egy nap a világ, directed by János Vaszary. Kárpát Film Kft., 1944.

Havi 200 fix, directed by Béla Balogh. Mozgóképipari Kft., 1936.

Hyppolit, a lakáj, directed by István Székely. Kovács Emil és Társa, Sonor Film, 1931.

Látta-e már Budapestet télen? directed by János Dáloky. Magyar Filmiroda, 1940.

Luci del varietà, directed by Alberto Lattuada and Federico Fellini. Capitolium, 1951.

Retour à l'aube, directed by Henri Decoin. Productions Bercholz, 1938.

Books, Book Chapters and Journal Articles

Adressbuch Internatinonaler Artistik (1943). Berlin-Dahlem: Wilhelm Ritter.

Alpár, Ágnes (1978). *A fővárosi kabarék műsora 1901–1944*, Budapest: Magyar Színházi Intézet.

Alpár, Ágnes (1981). *A fővárosi kabarék műsora 1945–1980*, Budapest: Magyar Színházi Intézet.

Balassa, Bela (1970). The economic reform in Hungary. *Economica*, New Series, 37 (February 145): 1–22.

Bercsényi, Tibor (1954). *Díszlettan*, Budapest: Felsőoktatási Jegyzetellátó.

Bogár, Richárd (n. d.). *Visszaemlékezések*. Manuscript, Országos Színházi Intézet Táncarchívuma.

Boldizsár, Iván (1956). *Hungary. A comprehensive guidebook for visitors and armchair travellers with many coloured illustrations and maps*, Budapest: Corvina.

Bozó, Péter (2020). Nationalism reloaded. Csínom Palkó by Ferenc Farkas in the light of sources of his estate, In Wolfgang Jansen ed. *Popular Music Theatre under Socialism. Operettas and Musicals in the Eastern European States 1945 to 1990*, 71–80. Populäre Kultur und Musik 30, Münster: Waxmann.

Bozó, Péter (2022). *Offenbach performance in Budapest 1920–1956. Orpheus on the Danube*, Cambridge: Cambridge University Press.
Brophy, John (1936). *Ilonka speaks of Hungary*, London: Hutchinson.
Cartledge, Bryan (2011). *The will to survive: A history of Hungary*, Oxford: Oxford University Press.
Czeizing, Lajos (1961). *Budapest bei Nacht – by Night – la Nuit*, Budapest: Corvina.
Dunai, Ákos (1984). *Magyar főnemesek az emigrációban*, Youngstown: Katolikus Magyarok Vasárnapja.
Edward (1951). *A king's story. The memoirs of H.R.H. the Duke of Windsor K. G.*, London: G. P. Putnam's Sons.
Elekes, Dezső (1938). *Budapest szerepe Magyarország szellemi életében*, Budapest: Budapest Székesfőváros Statisztikai Hivatala.
Fuchs, Lívia, Fügedi, János (2016). Doctrines and laban kinetography in a hungarian modern dance school in the 1930s. *Journal of Movement Arts Literacy* 3 (1): Article 3.
Gál, Róbert (2005). *Odavagyok magáért… Epizódok Fényes Szabolcs életéből.*, Budapest: K. u. K.
Gál, Róbert (2009). *Muzsikáló pesti éjszaka. A legendás EMKE zenés kávéház története*, Budapest: Rózsavölgyi és Társa.
Gáspár, Margit (1949). *Az operett*, Budapest: Népszava.
Glyn, Elinor (1932). *Love's Hour*, London: Duckworth.
Gyáni, Gábor (2004). Social history of Hungary in the horthy era. In Gábor Gyáni, György Kövér and Tibor Valuch eds. *Social History of Hungary from the Reform Era to the End of the Twentieth Century*, 271–507. Atlantic Studies on Society in Change No. 113. New York: Columbia University Press.
Gyarmati, György (2021). *A Rákosi-korszak. Rendszerváltó fordulatok évtizede Magyarországon, 1945–1956*, Budapest: Rubicon Intézet.
Havadi, Gergő (2008). Állambiztonság és a vendéglátás szigorúan ellenőrzött terei a szocializmusban. In Sándor Horváth, ed. *Mindennapok Rákosi és Kádár korában*, 172–186. Budapest: Nyitott Könyvműhely Kiadó.
Heltai, Gyöngyi (2011a). *Usages de l'opérette pendant la période socialiste en Hongrie 1949–1968*, Budapest: Atelier.
Heltai, Gyöngyi (2011b). A két háború közti operett stiláris és ideológiai dilemmái: A Király Színház példája (1921–1936) II. *Tánctudományi közlemények* 2011/2 pp. 33–74.
Heltai, Gyöngyi (2012). *Az operett metamorfózisai 1949–1956. A 'kapitalista giccs'-től a haladó 'mimusjáték'-ig*, Budapest: ELTE Eötvös.

Heltai, Gyöngyi (2013). A 'nevelő szórakoztatás' válsága 1954-ben: A bányász-operett és a Fővárosi Víg Színház bukása. http://real.mtak.hu/id/eprint/9322 Retrieved on 9 April 2023.

Heltai, Gyöngyi (2017). Színházi 'átállítás' – a pesti magánszínházi mező önszabályozó működési modelljének válsága, 1936–1942. Korall Társadalomtörténeti Folyóirat. 69. 94–126.

Heltai, Gyöngyi (2020). Hungarian operetta diplomacy 1955–1968. The case of Princess Csárdás. In Wolfgang Jansen ed., *Popular Music Theatre under Socialism. Operettas and Musicals in the Eastern European States 1945 to 1990*, 87–103. Populäre Kultur und Musik Vol. 30. Münster: Waxmann.

Heltai, Gyöngyi (2022). An American investor in the theatre industry of Budapest. Ben Blumenthal (1883–1967): A personal and professional biography. *Historical Studies on Central Europe* 2 (1): 162–89. https://doi.org/10.47074/HSCE.2022-1.08.

Hevesi, Endre (1948). *This is Hungary: A guide for tourists and armchair travellers*, Budapest: Athenaeum.

Jansen, Wolfgang ed. (2020). *Popular music theatre under socialism. Operettas and musicals in the eastern european states 1945 to 1990*. Populäre Kultur und Musik 30, Münster: Waxmann.

Kalmár, Melinda (2014). *Történelmi galaxisok vonzásában. Magyarország és a szovjetrendszer 1945–1990*, Budapest: Osiris.

Kalmár, Tibor (2013). *A humor háza. A Fészek Művészklub nagy mesélői*, Budapest: Kossuth.

Kalmár, Tibor (2015). *Sztárok az éjszakában*, Budapest: Kossuth.

Kappanyos, András (2017). Az ellenkultúra domesztikálása. In Ádám Ignácz ed. *Populáris zene és államhatalom*, 64–81. Budapest: Rózsavölgyi és Társa Kiadó.

Korossy, Zsuzsa (2007). Színházirányítás a Rákosi-korszak első felében. In Tamás Gajdó ed. *Színház és politika*, 45–139. Színháztudományi Szemle 37. Budapest: OSZMI.

Lewerenz, Susann (2014). The Tropical Express in Nazi Germany. In Len Platt, David Linton and Tobias Becker eds. *Popular Musical Theatre in London and Berlin*, 242–257. Cambridge: Cambridge University Press.

Mihályi, Péter (2018). *Rendszerváltás és elitcsere 1945 után. 70 éve történt a magyarországi gyáripar államosítása*. MTA Közgazdaság- és Regionális Tudományi Kutatóközpont Közgazdaság-tudományi Intézet Műhelytanulmányok MT-DP 2018/13.

Molnár Gál, Péter (2001). *A pesti mulatók*, Budapest: Helikon.

Molnár, Adrienne ed. (2004). *A 'hatvanas évek' emlékezete. Az Oral History Archívum gyűjteményéből*, Budapest: 1956-os Intézet.

Molnár, Dániel (2014). A játék vége – a pesti mulatók és varieték szabályozása 1945-től az államosításokig. In Károly Veress ed. *Játék és tudomány. Interdiszciplináris párbeszéd 2*, 125–142. Kolozsvár: Bolyai Társaság.

Molnár, Dániel (2017). Művészi elgondolás: Miss Arizona és Rozsnyai Sándor. Az Arizona Revue Dancing műsora és hatáskeltő elemei 1932–1944. *Replika*, 101–102, 89–118.

Molnár, Dániel (2019a). *Vörös csillagok. A Rákosi-korszak szórakoztatóipara és a szocialista revűk*, Budapest: Ráció.

Molnár, Dániel (2019b). 'A Whirlwind from the Puszta'. Hungarian and Hungarian style variety acts in Berlin, 1920–1961. In Izabela Kopania ed. *Acta Ethnographica Hungarica 64*. 211–226. Budapest: Akadémiai Kiadó.

Molnár, Dániel (2020). 'Revues have no allowances but requirements' – Set and costume design of the socialist revues in Budapest, 1949–1952. In Wolfgang Jansen ed. *Popular Music Theatre under Socialism. Operettas and Musicals in the Eastern European States 1945 to 1990*, 43–70. Populäre Kultur und Musik Vol. 30. Münster: Waxmann.

Molnár, Dániel (2021). 288 metres of velvet, 16 pairs of shoes, 12 yellow top hats, 5 bathtubs... – The staging and the cultural impact of the 1925 production of *Halló, Amerika!* in the Budapest Operetta Theatre. In Jernej Weiss ed. *Operetta between the Two World Wars*, 179–211. Studia musicologica Labacensia 5. Ljubljana: Festival Ljubljana.

Nagykovácsi, Ilona (1982). *Fény és árnyék*, Toronto: Vörösváry.

Nyári, László (1950). *Színházak szervezeti, szolgálati és fegyelmi szabályai; művészek, műszakiak és egyéb alkalmazottak illetmény-és nyugdíjügyei, valamint jogaik és kötelességeik*, Budapest: Népművelési Minisztérium Elnöki Főosztálya.

Odeschalchi, Eugénie (1987). *Egy hercegnő emlékezik*, Budapest: Gondolat.

Orlay, Jenő (1943). *Chappy – Jazzdobbal a világ körül*, Budapest.

Pöstenyi, Emőke (2020). *Das Fernsehballett. Mein Leben mit dem Tanz*, Berlin: Bild und Heimat.

Rajkai, György (1954). *Színpadtechnika*, Budapest: Felsőoktatási Jegyzetellátó.

Rácz, György (1984). *Mesterek árnyékában*, Budapest: Go-Press.

Rátonyi, Róbert (1984). *Operett II*, Budapest: Zeneműkiadó.

Rátonyi, Róbert (1987). *Mulató a Nagymező utcában*, Budapest: Idegenforalmi Propaganda és Kiadó Vállalat.

Romsics, Ignác (1999). *Hungary in the twentieth century*. Budapest: Corvina Osiris.

Simon, Géza Gábor (1992). *The book of Hungarian Jazz*, Budapest: Hotelinfo.

Simon, Géza Gábor (1999). *Magyar jazztörténet*, Budapest: Hotelinfo.

Statistical Pocket Book of Hungary 1960, Budapest: Közgazdasági és Jogi Kiadó.

Statistical Pocket Book of Hungary 1974, Budapest: Központi Statisztikai Hivatal.

Sugár, Róbert (1987). *Ugye, hogy nem felejtesz el?*, Zalaegerszeg: Ifjúsági Lap- és Könyvkiadó.

Szabó-Jilek, Iván (2022). A Maxim varieté tündöklése és bukása. In *Színpad* 2022/3. pp. 59–65. Budapest: Magyar Színháztechnikai Szövetség.

Szántó, Jenő (1933). A homosexualis férfiprostitutio kérdése. In *Népegészségügy* 1933/20–21. Budapest: Athenaeum.

Szántó, Judit ed. (1985). *A Művész Színház 1945–1949*. Almanach, Budapest: Múzsák.

Szívós, István, Uzoni, Ödön (1992): Az 1946-ban létrejött szovjet-magyar vegyes vállalatok. In *Valóság* 1992/1. pp. 67–85. Budapest: Tudományos Ismeretterjesztő Társulat.

Tarján, Vilmos (1940). *Pesti éjszaka*. Budapest: Általános nyomda, könyv- és lapkiadó Rt.

Valuch, Tibor (2004). Changes in the structure and lifestyle of the Hungarian society in the second half of the XXth century. In Gábor Gyáni, György Kövér and Tibor Valuch eds. *Social History of Hungary from the Reform Era to the end of the Twentieth Century*, 511–671. Atlantic Studies on Society in Change No. 113. New York: Columbia University Press.

Varga, Bálint András (1989). Hullámhegyek és hullámvölgyek – Székely Endre pályaképe. In *Muzsika* 1989/1. pp. 9–17. Budapest: Pro Musica Alapítvány.

Vay, Ilus (2006). *Miközben bohóckodtam*, Budapest: Duna Palota.

Vitányi, Iván (1965). *A 'könnyű műfaj'*, Budapest: Kossuth.

Zichy, Theodore (1974). *That was no gentleman – that was Zichy*, London: Polybooks.

Zipernovszky, Kornél (2020). 'Who will win – the jazz or Gypsy, it is hard to tell'. Gypsy musicians defend Hungarian national culture against American jazz. *AMERICANA – E-Journal of American Studies in Hungary*, Volume X, Special issue on jazz. http://americanaejournal.hu/vol10jazz/zipernovszky Retrieved on 9 April 2023.

Zsiray, Károly (1969). *A szocialista vendéglátóipar kialakulásának és fejlődésének története*. Unpublished manuscript, Magyar Kereskedelmi és Vendéglátóipari Múzeum Könyvtára.

Acknowledgements

This work could not have been done without those who helped my earlier book, *Vörös csillagok*. Nevertheless, I must express my heartfelt gratitude to Lilla Sebestyén and Stefan Kahn for making certain sources accessible to me and to the anonymous peer reviewers, whose comments and suggestions helped improve the quality of the text. I am indebted to William Everett, who found the subject and its questions as relevant as I did, and to my families in Berlin and Budapest, whose loving patience and support made this Element happen.

Cambridge Elements

Musical Theatre

William A. Everett
University of Missouri-Kansas City

William A. Everett, PhD is Curators' Distinguished Professor of Musicology at the University of Missouri-Kansas City Conservatory, where he teaches courses ranging from medieval music to contemporary musical theatre. His publications include monographs on operetta composers Sigmund Romberg and Rudolf Friml and a history of the Kansas City Philharmonic Orchestra. He is contributing co-editor of the *Cambridge Companion to the Musical* and the *Palgrave Handbook of Musical Theatre Producers*. Current research topics include race, ethnicity and the musical and London musical theatre during the 1890s.

About the Series
Elements in Musical Theatre focus on either some sort of "journey" and its resulting dialogue or on theoretical issues. Since many musicals follow a quest model (a character goes in search of something), the idea of a journey aligns closely to a core narrative in musical theatre. Journeys can be, for example, geographic (across bodies of water or land masses), temporal (setting musicals in a different time period than the time of its creation), generic (from one genre to another), or personal (characters in search of some sort of fulfilment). Theoretical issues may include topics relevant to the emerging scholarship on musical theatre from a global perspective and can address social, cultural, analytical and aesthetic perspectives.

Cambridge Elements

Musical Theatre

Elements in the Series

A Huge Revolution of Theatrical Commerce: Walter Mocchi and the Italian Musical Theatre Business in South America
Matteo Paoletti

The Empire at the Opéra: Theatre, Power and Music in Second Empire Paris
Mark Everist

"Why Aren't They Talking?": The Sung-Through Musical from the 1980s to the 2010s
Alex Bádue

Offenbach Performance in Budapest, 1920–1956: Orpheus on the Danube
Péter Bozó

West Side Story in Spain: The Transcultural Adaptation of an Iconic American Show
Paul R. Laird and Gonzalo Fernández Monte

Kickstarting Italian Opera in the Andes: The 1840s and the First Opera Companies
José Manuel Izquierdo König

Singing Zarzuela, 1896–1958: Approaching Portamento and Musical Expression through Historical Recordings
Eva Moreda Rodríguez

The Revue in Twentieth-Century Budapest: From Cosmopolitan Nightclubs to Stalinist Dogma
Dániel Molnár

A full series listing is available at: www.cambridge.org/EIMT

For EU product safety concerns, contact us at Calle de José Abascal, 56–1°,
28003 Madrid, Spain or eugpsr@cambridge.org.

www.ingramcontent.com/pod-product-compliance
Ingram Content Group UK Ltd.
Pitfield, Milton Keynes, MK11 3LW, UK
UKHW020852180525
458533UK00014B/204